Oman

MUIYUEN

• Waiyeung

TUNGKWUN

WAIYEUNG

HOIFUNG→

PO ON

Pinghai •

Shumchun •

Shekou •

NEW TERRITORIES

HONG KONG

KOWLOON

Lantau
Island

HONG KONG
ISLAND

N

0   4   8   12   16   20 km

0   2   4   6   8   10   12 mi

# In Times of
# GREAT CHAOS

Compiled by
## CHRISTA TISDALL

with an introduction by
## JAN MORRIS

*Contributors:*
David Bonavia   Father Sean Burke   Anthony Lawrence   Bea Hutcheon
Margaret Ng   Ann Quon   Nancy Ma Thompson   Sybil Wong

# Introduction

This book perpetuates the memories of thirty-eight people destined to live their lives in circumstances of chaos — chaos of poverty, chaos of war, chaos of uncertainty. Most of them were born in China before the first world war — some rich, some poor. All have ended up poor in Hong Kong during the last years of British colonial rule.

Consider the brutal sequence of events into which these men and women have been seized. In 1911 when many of them were children, the Ching dynasty was overthrown. In the late Twenties, China was plunged into civil conflict between rival ideologies. In 1937 the Japanese invaded China, gradually embroiling most of the country in war. In 1941 they invaded Hong Kong, throwing out its British rulers and reducing it to miserable indigence. In 1949 the Communists gained control of China, changing every aspect of the national life and driving hundreds of thousands of people into exile. In the 1960s Hong Kong, by a combination of ruthless enterprise and untrammelled *laissez faire*, turned itself by hook and by crook into a great industrial power. In 1984 London and Beijing reached agreement on the future of Hong Kong. In 1997 the colony will return apprehensively to Chinese rule.

There could hardly be a historical period more unremittingly stressful for its participants, in a part of the world more unforgivingly demanding. Many of the contributors to this book have experienced it all. In the ballot of life no straws could be drawn much shorter and yet they have lived to tell the tale in these pages with composure and frequently with humour. From the terrors of war in childhood to the pressures of capitalist society in old age, they have spent their whole lives fighting a tough destiny. It is no wonder that sometimes they have relied upon drugs and illegalities to see them through; more amazing by far that so often, to judge by their recollections here, they have retained such balance of mind and serenity.

They have had few allies in their varied and often fascinating battles of life. However in their later years they have found kindness, support and comradeship from Helping Hand, in whose aid this book is published.

It is a non-profit concern, set up specifically to care for elderly Hong Kong Chinese with neither funds nor families to support them; so that 'In Times of Great Chaos' is happily the expression not only of a generation's harsh struggle, but of friendship in the end.

**Jan Morris**

*" In times of great chaos*
*one should live in the country;*
*in times of minor unrest*
*one should live in the town. "*

Published by Helping Hand Limited, 12 Borrett Road, 1st Floor, Hong Kong

ISBN 962-7373-01-X

Typeset by AB Studio, Hong Kong
Colour separations by Tenon & Polert, Hong Kong
Printed and bound by Everbest Printing Company Limited, Hong Kong
Printed in Hong Kong.

**Editors' note:** In keeping with the times of these stories, place names appear as they were then in common use, with transliterations following the Cantonese or South China pronunciations. Apart from a few personal names, other Chinese words are similarly transliterated.

The wars and upheavals through which the storytellers lived are listed chronologically, along with major events, in the historical background on page 127. Notes on the ethnic groups mentioned by the storytellers are on the same page.

Guidance on geography and topography is given in the endpaper maps. The first shows the Pearl River delta area of Kwangtung Province and the one at the end of the book covers most of China.

# Contents

# *Foreword*

Helping Hand was founded in 1978 to provide shelter and care for the homeless elderly of Hong Kong. Since then the voluntary agency has helped to rehouse more than five thousand old people. It now manages fifteen homes, the most recent ones providing full-time nursing care.

This book has been produced to introduce some of the men and women whom the people of Hong Kong have so generously supported over the past ten years. They appear in these pages not necessarily because they have exceptional stories to tell, but because they willingly came forward to share their memories with us. Most of them — not all — would claim to be ordinary people who have led what seem to them to be ordinary lives. But they have one thing in common: they are all survivors — survivors of years of turmoil in China and, indeed, Hong Kong. We cannot vouch for the veracity of their stories, nor for the accuracy of all the information they contain. There have inevitably been lapses of memory and, perhaps sometimes, a dash of make-believe. We have translated, shaped and edited the often fragmented interviews. But in the end we have told the stories as they were told to us.

Many people helped with the production of this book. Lui Man-chi, whose story is the first to appear, is also the artist responsible for the calligraphy at the beginning of each story and it is to him that we would first like to extend our thanks and appreciation. Our particular thanks go to the late David Bonavia, Anthony Lawrence, Father Sean Burke, Bea Hutcheon, Margaret Ng, Ann Quon, Nancy Thompson and Sybil Wong, who, with myself, conducted the interviews, many of which I then converted into the stories which appear in this book. Derek Davies, Father Denis Hanly and Shirley Sherrard read some of the manuscripts and made many helpful suggestions. All stories were finally edited by Joyce Savidge and David K. Lewis. Thanks are due to Anthony Iun and interpreters from the Royal Hong Kong Police Force and also to students from the Hong Kong Polytechnic who translated tape-recordings in their spare time. The photographer responsible for most of the portraits and pictures in this book wishes to remain anonymous. We owe him much. Keith MacGregor kindly contributed the photographs on pages 11, 14 and 120. The endpaper maps were prepared by Dr Richard Irving of the Geography Department of Hong Kong University and Mr Robert Upton, of the Government Secretariat, assisted with the difficult task of identifying places. For design and production of the book we are indebted to Peter Cook, Sue Tickner and their staff. Beth Gubersky gave invaluable advice on publishing and distribution. Maggie Carter put the whole package together. To these and many others who gave so generously of their time and skills and in particular to Jan Morris for her Introduction, we are deeply grateful.

Finally we must thank the men and women who allowed us to tell their stories. They and the many others who live in our homes have made our efforts not only worthwhile but so very enjoyable.

**Christa Tisdall**

# *No compensation*

呂
文
熾

**I** was born in 1911, the second child in a family of three sons and three daughters. My father was in the tobacco business in Hong Kong, working for my maternal grandfather. My mother's family had money. Their house in Canton was big and we visited them often.

My mother was very beautiful. She had bound feet, but not too small — not as small as her sister's. And she was very well educated. She opened a girls' school in our village in Sunwui County and she was its headmistress. In those days few girls went to school. My mother was indeed unusual. Everyone in the village respected her.

I was raised and went to school in the village. In those days life was better and more comfortable in the countryside. And the rich lived well. At twenty-four I was married. My parents died that year, both within the same month. They were in their fifties. In those days that was quite old — not like now, when we all live on to be seventy or even eighty.

When Japan invaded China, some two years later, I joined the anti-Japanese guerrilla forces in Sunwui run by the Kuomintang. I was recruited by my brother-in-law who was the commander of the KMT forces in the area. I went along to help. During the war what else was there to do?

I was with the guerrilla forces for eight years, in charge of supplies and provisions. Grain, clothing, uniforms, ammunition — all had to be procured somehow. It was very difficult and corruption was rampant. The ammunition given to us by the army often didn't fit our guns. So we had to find other types of guns or different ammunition.

Organising food supplies was a nightmare. In the beginning, some places were better off for food than others, but in the end all were short. Chungshan was the best place and we went there twice a year to buy grain. The mayor was responsible for finding it for us and we would then give it to the local miller to grind. The villagers kept the husks. Village elders were responsible for the provision of vegetables, fish and meat.

In some areas people had so little that after they had supplied the army they were left with nothing. That's why so many people died of hunger. Tungkwun was the worst, but people were starving everywhere. What could we do? There was not enough food, the Japanese were bombing us and the army went hungry too. Even the Japanese soldiers were in bad shape. We saw them through our binoculars. They dug in on mountain tops, and their clothes were torn and ragged.

I came to Hong Kong in 1949 with my adopted daughter. Her father had been with the guerrillas and had no means of supporting her. My wife and I were childless so I said 'Give her to me and I will raise her'. He was a common soldier and glad to know she was being provided for.

My wife did not come with me to Hong Kong. We had a noodle shop in Canton and she stayed there to look after the business; she died in 1950. I later married my adopted daughter's mother, whose husband was killed in the war. You want to know what happened to her? Well, she returned to China for a visit one day, but when she wanted to come back to Hong Kong they had closed

*Lui Man-chi*

the border and she was not allowed in. She had a lot of trouble in her village. A nephew of hers was arrested — I never quite understood why — and she was detained as well. I sent money every month to support her. She died four years ago.

When I first came to Hong Kong I worked in a spinning factory. Later I opened a small tea-house in Wanchai which I had for many years. I also ran a roast meat shop. Sunwui, where I come from, is famous for its roast meat.

I was Secretary of the Hong Kong Committee for Compensation and Claims against the Japanese for twelve years from 1969 to 1980. I ran the whole organisation. There were several thousand claims. In the beginning some Japanese officials came to see us and said 'Wait, just wait, and we will see what we can do'. They used delaying tactics. I then led about a thousand claimants to the Japanese Consulate General. The Consul General agreed to accept the claims but, after waiting a long time, nothing happened. Everyone lost heart. We got no compensation at all!

At that time I lived in a two-storey hut in Tsuenwan. When the government demolished the hut, I and my daughter and her family moved to Tsing Yi, where we had a public housing flat. My daughter had three children. Sadly, we had some disagreement. Also her husband worked elsewhere and transport was inconvenient. So they moved out. After my daughter moved away I was allowed to stay in the flat for one year by myself, which was very considerate of the authorities. But later I had to move because the flat was classed as too big for one person. That's why I came to this home. My youngest grandchild — who's now eighteen — comes to see me regularly. He brings me food and goes to the movies with me.

I depend on Public and Old Age Assistance. Although I'm eighty-seven my health is good. It is convenient here — the market is just outside. I cook for myself. I get up at about six o'clock in the morning and do some exercises to loosen my joints. I make breakfast, read the papers, shop for food and cook for some of the people here. I like to write and do Chinese drawings — it passes the time very well. I began drawing here in this home. I had never done it before, but I borrowed a book on painting and calligraphy and taught myself. There are fifteen Helping Hand homes for the elderly and towards New Year I always take brush and paper and do good luck characters for all of them. I also write letters for people. Many of the people in this home are illiterate and it would cost them six dollars to have a letter written outside.

On Sundays I go to church. I am a Catholic. You ask why I became a Catholic? Ah, that's an interesting story. Three years ago, I was very ill. First my stomach bled and then the lining of my brain got inflamed — my nerves seized up. I was unable to get out of bed for two months. Three times I was in Princess Margaret Hospital. During this time a woman friend looked after me. She was a Catholic and one day she brought a priest to visit me. My stomach and back hurt very badly that day and I was in terrible pain. The priest prayed for me and suddenly all the pain was gone. When he had finished praying I had no pain at all. Believe it or not — I have had no more problems since I was baptised last year. God looks after me now.

# *Am I not fortunate?*

I have been lucky for most of my life. My father spoiled me, my husband was good to me and my daughters look after me. I was born in 1912, the first of four children. We lived in Shuntak County, near to Canton, and my father was rich. He owned a company that packed and shipped goods overseas. I felt very close to my father and he loved me too. Every morning before I went to school he would call for me and he would plait my hair. He would bring me sweets and laugh with me. I was his favourite child; he loved me more than his son.

When I was five I started learning to read and write characters. In those days it was unusual for a daughter to be taught, so I consider myself lucky. Unfortunately I am very stupid and have forgotten it all. I can't remember anything. What a shame to have wasted my father's good money.

I was married when I was eighteen. It was a blind marriage arranged by a marriage-broker. A mutual friend told my father that the boy was very nice, had a good family background and a fine house in Canton. My father insisted on seeing the title deeds before the agreement was made. He wanted to confirm that all was in order and that I would be well provided for. Then we were betrothed. I was sent away to my grandmother and the families began to exchange presents in ceremonies that went on for ten days.

It was all done in grand style and I remember it well. The family of the bridegroom sent more than two hundred cakes, dried seafood and mushrooms. There were two cakes in each basket and *laisee* packets containing a 'dragon cent' and peanuts — which are considered very lucky because of the sound of their name, *hua sheng*. My family sent baskets of fruit in return.

On the day before the wedding my dowry was carried by porters to my in-laws' house. My father was very generous. All the Shuntak people in Canton commented on this. Part of my dowry was a large set of redwood tables and chairs inlaid with marble. Those alone cost several hundred dollars. There was also bedding, mosquito nets, curtains, a carved cupboard, a camphorwood chest full of clothes, bowls, plates, cups — even two pipes for smoking.

On the following day, I was carried in the bridal sedan-chair to my in-laws' house, taking more presents and boxes of cakes. That night the bridegroom's family held a wedding banquet for over three hundred people. I wore the *kwa* — the red bridal gown. Two women guided me around the tables. I served tea and bowed. It was all very tiring and at the end of the day my feet were swollen. There were so many mothers-in-law. Didn't I tell you? I had six mothers-in-law and I was their first daughter-in-law.

My father gave a big party the same evening which I did not attend. Through his business he knew many people and had a name to uphold. It was a lavish wedding — I know that he spent well over three thousand silver dollars, and that was a great deal of money in those days. But both families were wealthy. However, the world is chaotic and, as you can see, I now have nothing left at all. It is hard to know what lies in the future.

My father-in-law dealt in Chinese porcelain and antiques and my husband worked for him. I

*Lee Man-jun*

went to the shop quite often, but I didn't really learn very much. Antiques seem far too boring when you're young. I was happy in my marriage. My husband treated me very well — really he was a model husband. When I was twenty we had a daughter and then another girl was born when I was twenty-three. But only a few months after her birth my husband fell ill. I don't know what the sickness was but no medicine could cure him and he died. I was a widow at the age of twenty-three.

At the time people said that I should get married again. But I thought that I would not bother. If I married and it didn't work out, it would be worse than being alone with my daughters. I decided to work and to support my daughters and myself. Because my husband's mother was not the senior wife in the household, and as I had only produced daughters, there was little interest in myself or my girls. So I left them with my mother and came to Hong Kong, where I found a job very quickly.

For the next few years I worked as a maid, eventually earning five dollars a month. In those days the going rate was only three, but I was paid much more because I worked well and my employers wanted to keep me. They even took me with them to Shanghai, where we stayed during most of the Japanese occupation. Towards the end of the war we moved to Canton, where they still owned a large house. They let me have my daughters live with me there — the youngest was ten by then. And I was able to help my parents with money.

After the war I followed my employers back to Hong Kong. There was a bit of a problem as the People's Liberation Army did not want to let my daughters go. Finally I told them that I was only the girls' foster-mother and that I was taking them to Hong Kong to search for their father. After three days I got a permit. Later, after my father died, I managed to bring my mother out as well. We were very lucky. We missed all the *Saam Fan* and *Ng Fan* campaigns — the 'Three Antis' and the 'Five Antis', which told people the things they should be against. There was such chaos in China.

My elder daughter was married in Hong Kong in 1950. The younger stayed with me for a while and then married at the age of twenty. I worked until I was in my sixties. Then my daughters told me to retire. They said that I was getting skinny and that they would look after me. By this time I had been with my second employer for twenty-one years.

After I stopped working I lived with my younger daughter. Then our stone hut was going to be torn down and my daughter's family was allocated public housing. Because I was not registered as a resident I was not allowed to join them. Now the rules have changed. They are always changing.

One of my daughters lives in Chaiwan, which is very near here. It's most convenient and I often go to have a cup of soup — or, when the weather is cold, to have a bath. I have seven grandchildren and even some great grandchildren. Every Sunday I take tea with them. Am I not fortunate? I had a happy childhood, a good marriage and have very considerate children. My parents looked after me and I cared for them when they needed me. I looked after my daughters and now they look after me. It is as it should be.

# You can't play mahjong with welfare money

**I** am a native of Pinghai in Waiyeung County. My family were poor peasants. We leased our land and paid our rent in kind. I had one sister who was three years younger than me. When she was seven my parents gave her to a cousin in a neighbouring village who had no children of her own. But later that cousin died and her in-laws sold my sister. She was sixteen or seventeen years old then and, although we looked for her, we never saw her again.

I never went to school; there was no money. So, as I grew older, I helped my father in the fields. But when I was about eighteen my father died and the landowner refused to let me continue to farm the land. To support my mother I did all sorts of odd jobs, hiring myself out to farmers in the villages around. I never had the time or money to find myself a wife. I lived from day to day.

My mother died when I was about thirty. Soon afterwards I came to Hong Kong. It was easy in those days. You got on the Pinghai ferry in the evening, ate dinner on board and you'd arrive in Shaukeiwan the next morning. I had no family in Hong Kong but I found work simply by asking around. People would want to know what I could do and I told them that I was strong and could tackle any physical work. For more than a year I carried sand, which is quite dangerous work: you carry heavy baskets off a lighter, walking down an unsteady gangplank. But the pay was good — seven dollars a day. I packed it in in the end because of the cold — you had to walk through the water to get onto the gangplank and in the winter it was icy!

For the next thirty-seven years I worked as a coolie for the utility companies in Hong Kong, digging ditches for gas and water pipes and for electric cables. However, it wasn't a full-time job. Like most of my friends I went from company to company wherever there was work. When it rained we didn't work and got no money, although if the boss was in a good mood, he would give us ten dollars to buy food; but often there was no pay at all.

There was one good thing though: while on the job you did get accommodation. There would be anywhere between twenty to forty people in the rooms we slept in. You'd find yourself a space and roll out your mat; there were no beds. We'd eat out at the cooked food stalls. Nowadays it is different. No one gives you a place to sleep any more but the pay is better: eighty, ninety even up to a hundred dollars a day for casual labour; but finding a bed is hard.

I'm seventy-five now. When I was sixty-eight I was told I wasn't going to be given any more work because of my age. I asked my employers to allow me to continue. After all, sixty-eight is not terribly old and I was in good health. But they refused.

After I became unemployed I used to sleep in the streets or on benches in places like Victoria Park. I picked up the odd job here and there but I didn't earn enough to fill my belly. Then I had an accident. I hurt my head badly and had to spend time in hospital. Just before I was discharged, a doctor talked to me and when he learned that I had no money and nowhere to go, he gave me sixty dollars and a note to a social worker to try and find me a place to stay.

So, yes, I actually have a home now, a room to live in. This is much better than digging ditches.

*Cheung Ming*

Nobody is driving me away at night any more. You know, I have even learned to cook and how to use an electric rice cooker. I shop for my own food, and if I am careful, there is enough for my needs — two meals a day. Mostly I eat bean curd, tomatoes and fish. I can't eat anything hard because I have no teeth. Social Welfare tells me I can apply to get false teeth, but it seems too much trouble. So I haven't bothered.

I can't read, so I spend a lot of time watching television. I also help grow flowers which I enjoy very much. I get seven hundred and eighty-five dollars a month from Social Welfare. You can't play mahjong with welfare money so I never do. I go walking every morning just to pass the time.

Yes, life is better now than it has ever been before. For me, just to survive is a luxury.

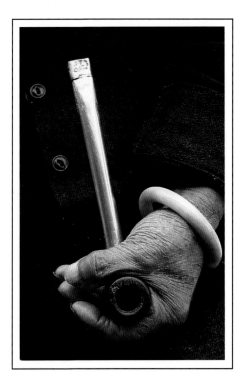

# *The bomb changed everything*

**C**ome a little closer and talk louder. My eyes are not so good and I'm almost deaf. Well, what can you expect? I'm eighty-three this year. My arms are not good either — can't lift anything heavy. But that's not because of old age. It happened a long time ago, after the war when I had to go out to make a living for myself.

I never had to look for a job until then. When I was a little girl, growing up in Hong Kong, I used to help my father in his grocery store — especially when my two brothers went to school. Times were different then. Girls didn't go to school and by the time I was sixteen I was married. It wasn't that I didn't have a lot to do. I took care of my husband, his parents and the five children who came as the years passed. But I never had to go outside the home to find work until after the bomb. The bomb changed everything.

It happened early in the morning. I had gone to the public toilet in Central. People didn't have toilets in their homes in those days. The planes flew over very fast, dropped their bombs and flew away. I ran home and when I got there nothing was left, just rubble! My husband, my mother-in-law and father-in-law and my five children all died when the bomb hit our home.

Afterwards I went to live with my own mother and father and older brother. Soon the soldiers came. There was fighting in the streets and my older brother was killed. It was then that my parents decided to return to their native village in China. It was up in the mountains and safe from the war. I didn't want to go to a mountain village on the mainland and I stayed behind in Hong Kong. But things got worse when the Japanese army took over. There was no work, no food and no medicine. Finally I fled and began walking towards Macau, where my youngest brother lived.

It was a long walk to Macau. When I set out I was all alone. But I met many people along the way who were fleeing in the same direction. We went through the mountains, avoiding the big towns and the soldiers. At night we found shelter in old abandoned temples that were scattered through the countryside. Nobody had food with them. We begged from farmers all along the way. Sometimes we got food but most of the time we just went hungry. I stayed with my brother and his family for a time; but with their seven children I was a burden on the family and so I returned to Hong Kong at the end of the war.

When I got back I had to find work to support myself. Food was rationed, the streets were full of refugees from China and there was no place to live. I moved into a broken-down hut on Wellington Street. It wasn't much — just a shelter against the weather — but I lived in it for twenty years. At first I sold firewood to make a living: getting up early each morning, going out to the hillsides, scrounging around for scraps of wood, binding them up with string, carrying them back into town and then looking for people to sell the bundles to. I did this for five years. That's when my arms gave out.

Fortunately I later found a job in a godown in Quarry Bay, as a gatekeeper and caretaker. I was paid about forty-five dollars a month, which was enough to feed myself. During this time, someone from my family's village in the mountains came and told me that my parents had died. When the

*Lou Shun-lin*

government tore down my shack on Wellington Street, I found a hut in Junk Bay. It had a bit of soil around it and I grew some vegetables and raised some chickens. By then I was sixty and had to retire from the job at the godown. After that I just walked around picking up whatever odd jobs I could find to keep body and soul together.

About three years ago, when I was eighty, they tore down my hut in Junk Bay too. Some friends helped me get on Public Assistance. Then they got me this place to live. You know, I just paid a doctor five hundred and ten dollars to cure this cough of mine. Can you imagine? Five hundred and ten dollars! You raise a family when you're young so that when you're old you will have somebody to take care of you. But the bomb changed that. The bomb changed everything.

# *How illusions died*

I was born in Shanghai in 1920, which makes me 68 today. My father was a coal merchant, well-to-do, and we lived in the British concession. I graduated from Shanghai YMCA High School and went on to study Political Economy at the University of Nanking. The school was run by British and American missionaries. I myself am a Christian; I was baptised at college in America.

As a student, I was supported financially by my father. After the Japanese war began, he moved to Hong Kong where he was employed by the Nationalist Government as a senior official in their Trade Mission. He died just before the Japanese attacked Pearl Harbour. My mother had died long before. I didn't realise it at the time, but perhaps they were fortunate.

My younger sister stayed behind in Shanghai. She had Communist sympathies and I believe she joined the Communist underground. She became a primary school teacher after the war and is now retired in Shanghai. As for myself, I have always been non-partisan in politics. Yes, it is true I have worked for both the Nationalists and the Communists. But I never joined either party. I have always looked at politics more from a philosophical than a political point of view.

During the war I joined the Kuomintang army and rose to the rank of lieutenant-colonel. But as you know, during some of those years the Nationalists and Communists were officially co-operating in the fight against the Japanese. There were always Communist agents within the KMT army and we all got to know each other very well. We shared some hopes and ideals.

After the Japanese surrendered, I returned to Shanghai where I worked as a city news reporter and as a translator for the United Nations Rehabilitation Programme. Later I took a government examination and qualified to study in the United States. I was sent to the Virginia Military Institute which included military training in its curriculum. I studied liberal arts. It was at the university that I became a Christian — a member of the Presbyterian Church. It all happened because of an American girl. She sang in the church choir and I liked her very much.

We had to pay our own way. My father had left me some money, the house in Shanghai and some land which I sold. It was not much, but enough to pay for my studies. When the Communists began to gain control in China my financial situation became difficult. I was also very anxious to get some of my family out of Shanghai; so I left the States to return to China. But I was too late. Shanghai had already fallen to the Communists and I found myself trapped in Hong Kong.

At first I found employment as a translator; I had no Hong Kong qualifications which would enable me to take up a profession. Later I approached some of my Communist party contacts. At first they didn't want to admit that they knew me. But eventually I was given a job on the Chinese-language New Evening Post where I remained as one of their chief columnists for more than fifteen years. I was the sole author of their poems praising Chairman Mao and his Thoughts.

Do you know — I was probably the first person ever to talk about 'Ping-Pong diplomacy'. This was in January 1971 when — at the invitation of the US-financed University Service Centre — I addressed a group of American scholars. I predicted that there would soon be a 'thaw' between

*Peter Chiang*

China and the United States. I suggested that this newly developing relationship should not be confined to cultural and scientific exchanges but that there should also be sports teams visiting each other's country. A beginning could be made with the exchange of Ping-Pong players, I said. This speech was very well received and much commented on.

Unfortunately, that same year my life took a turn for the worse. At that time China was in ideological turmoil and people were drifting blindly from right to left. I had serious disagreements with my employers, followed by a very unpleasant experience. I found myself arrested for the alleged possession of dangerous drugs. This was a frame-up. Luckily, some highly respected Hong Kong citizens vouched for my personal integrity. The case against me, so obviously pointless and contrived, was dismissed.

I decided to change my way of life. I obtained a teaching permit from the Education Department which enabled me to teach in private secondary schools. I taught English, Geography, History and Civics. I first taught in Kowloon and then for ten years worked and lived in the New Territories.

Private school teachers only earn about one-third of what teachers at government schools are paid. When I was last employed I made less than three thousand dollars a month and most of that went on rent, food and transport. I had no savings at all.

When I retired I went straight to the Social Welfare Department and they made Public Assistance available to me. I am not proud. I also applied for the Government Single Housing Scheme and, as a result, I shall soon be living in a housing estate.

I have returned to the mainland twice: first in 1977 and then again in 1981. I saw quite a number of my old teachers and schoolmates. They had all suffered badly during the Cultural Revolution. My sister also suffered greatly. She told me that all the teachers were subjected to 'struggle' meetings. They had to accuse one another, criticise and self-criticise. There was much tension and fear. People became spiteful. Friend turned against friend.

My sister wrote many forced confessions. How many she can't remember. Not that they made any difference. She was denounced for 'Capitalist and Revisionist' tendencies. She was publicly humiliated and beaten up by the Red Guards. The neighbours, too, pushed her around and beat her. She was forced to retire and never worked again. My sister's husband, also a teacher, was deported for 'reform through labour', as it was called in those days. Her children were scattered all over Manchuria, north-west China and Tsinghai. Of her family only her husband was allowed back to Shanghai. The children never returned. After years in the countryside there were no jobs for them in Shanghai. They have no skills, no knowledge, no education at all. You need to have connections in China.

My sister was later rehabilitated. She received some compensation and in 1980 was allocated a small flat under the reforms of Deng Xiao-ping. But she never worked again.

When I was young I used to have illusions. I hoped that Mao Tse-tung and his government would do something for the Chinese people. They had suffered so much: long years of civil war, the Japanese war, the World War, and then civil war again — people were so tired of it all. It was for that reason that they put their hope in a strong new government. I fear, however, that most Chinese, young and old, were sooner or later disillusioned.

Things seem to be improving now. During my train trips through China I observed that people were working and carrying goods both day and night. There is food in the markets and restaurants are opening again. Things were stagnant under Mao. Now the countryside seems to have come alive again.

I am not very sure what the future of Hong Kong will be; but I don't think that the Communists will kill the goose that lays the golden egg. When I first came to Hong Kong it was a poor city; but over the years it has grown very strong in many ways. I think that Communist visitors to Hong Kong have learned something here.

Today I spend my time reading. I borrow books from the public library — one of my favourite writers is Graham Greene. I also enjoy reading the Sherlock Holmes detective stories. I studied German for one year. I fear I have forgotten most of it but I still enjoy German literature in translation. I read Goethe's Faust and the philosophers Kant and Schopenhauer. I also enjoy Bach and Beethoven.

I have friends in Germany. They tell me that life there is quite good — even better than in Hong Kong. Not so many robbers and beggars! They also tell me that the situation in East Germany is very bad. The trouble with the Communists is that they put the cart before the horse all the time. That is not the real Materialism as it was taught by Marx and Engels.

# *My father sold me*

**E**ver since I was a young girl, life has been very hard for me. When I was a child my father did have some money. But he was an opium smoker and he fell into bad company. Year after year our life became more difficult.

I was born in the Year of the Dragon, in 1904. My sister was the lucky one. She was born two years before me, in the Year of the Tiger. When she was married to a wealthy Toishan farmer my father gave her a really grand wedding. Four thousand wedding cakes were sent out. There was a banquet with three hundred guests. She was given bedding and furniture. She had everything!

When it was my turn, only two years later, my father had very little money left. But you'll never believe what he did. He didn't marry me off — he sold me off. Yes, he sold me, his second daughter, for two hundred and twenty yuan to a peasant family. Not much, you may say, but it was more than a labourer would earn in a year. At first, I refused to go. I cried and pleaded with my parents. But it was no good. They wouldn't give me food any more. They beat me. They pushed me out of the house. I had no choice but to go.

I had a son when I was eighteen or nineteen and then a daughter. Or perhaps it was the girl first; I can't remember. My husband left before the second baby was born. He went overseas to find work. He never saw the baby. He never came back. In those days there were many bandits in the countryside. They came to our village, robbed us and set fire to our house. My sister's husband's house was gone. We had nowhere to live and all our food was gone. Both my children died of hunger, and so did my father.

Some time after the death of my children I married an old man who had come back from America. I married him because I was hungry and he had some money. He was in his sixties and, in fact, quite crazy. But I didn't care — I needed to eat. The old man brought me to Hong Kong and for a while we lived in peace. Then the Japanese came and we walked back to our village in Toishan. But the Japanese came to the village as well. Again there was famine and my husband died. Many others starved as well — mainly small children and old people like my husband. His money was no use to him in the end.

I had to work hard to survive the next few years. I sold *congee* and drinks, I swept the streets and cut grass. It was all very heavy work, but it barely made a living. After the Communists took over life got even worse. Again there was no food. My brother, his wife and their children all died of starvation. Many of my sister's family died as well. I decided to get away to Hong Kong by boat, but we were robbed by pirates and I arrived here with absolutely nothing. Then I could find no work and so finally I walked back to China.

After the Cultural Revolution I applied to come back to Hong Kong once again. I said that I had family here and, as I was elderly, I was given an exit permit without much trouble. It was easier to find work this time and I even had enough to sometimes send a little money back to my sister — she who'd had so grand a wedding!

For a while I worked as an amah looking after children. Then I worked in a garment factory.

*Chan Lin-tai*

After that I had a job in a restaurant; I washed dishes, swept the floors, peeled the prawns — all the dirty work. Look, my fingers are all crooked from working, but still I'm lucky as I have no rheumatism in my limbs.

After I turned seventy-five the Social Welfare Department started taking care of me. I was given a bed in this home and some money. My life now is ten times better than before. But I think, when I am very old, I will go back to China.

# *A risky business*

**L**ook at me now: I was a strong man once. Six feet tall and weighing over 180 pounds. Today all my strength is gone, my health is poor, my muscles are wasting. No, I'm not asking for your sympathy. I'm not complaining, nor do I feel sorry for myself. Many of my friends are old and wasted just like me. I'm now seventy-five.

My parents were Tanka people. I was born on the family fishing junk in Aberdeen and as a boy I worked on it. But several brothers were born after me, and then there were too many of us for the boat. So when I was twelve my parents found work for me on a junk in Aberdeen.

It was a good job; but those junks moved with the winds and we were always at the mercy of sea and weather. Sometimes, the sky would swallow the winds and we would lie idle for days. Then a storm would blow up and we would have to find shelter. Luckily, we didn't have to go far for a good catch in those days. We would set sail before dawn and return to Aberdeen in the evening. As we drew near the quay, the buyers would be waiting for us. Catches were heavy — running into tons; we took both large and small fish in our trawl nets.

There were no fishermen's co-operatives then. Fish was plentiful and cheap. I was making about thirty dollars a month and never thought of doing anything else. Then came the Japanese. Life in Hong Kong became very harsh. People were starving. So I left and went to Macau. I found work on a boat smuggling *mui* — tiny shrimps made into fish paste — into China. We would buy them very cheaply, in Tai O on Lantau, and take them to Heungchow in Chinese territory. Our boats were so small — even when the moon was full, you could hardly spot them.

Once in China, we would sell the shrimps and buy rice and sweet potatoes. There was plenty of rice along the South China coast; but almost none in Hong Kong or Macau. People were starving on *congee* — that is why we became smugglers.

It was dangerous work. The Japanese had banned the export of *mui* shrimp. Had we been caught by them we would have been put in jail — or shot. We were pretty lucky though. Several times we were captured by the Chinese Militia working for the Japanese. They had bigger and faster boats and they knew where to look for us. When they caught us, they would confiscate all we had. Then they would beat us up. Once I was beaten really badly — the blows rained down on my body. I thought I was never going to see morning again.

It was after that beating that I decided to return to Hong Kong to look for my family. But both my parents had died. My father had been clubbed to death by the Chinese Militia who caught him stealing food. My mother had passed away soon after. I hung around and was picked up by the Japanese who sent me to a camp at Victoria Barracks. When I was released a few weeks later I was just skin and bones. I went back to Tai O and started smuggling again. I knew the dangers of being caught. But, damn it, if you are hungry you do anything to find food.

Finally the war ended. The Japanese left and life improved a bit; but not really very much. Food was both scarce and expensive. Smuggling still seemed like a reasonable way to make a living — and so I remained at sea.

*Lai Fook*

You must understand: in those days, China was terribly poor. Later, there was a ban on taking many kinds of goods and materials to the mainland. My friends and I smuggled steel. We would set out late at night with two or three sampans in a convoy, each carrying cargo worth thirty or forty thousand dollars. A man from the China side — we called him the headman — would go with us. We rowed straight to Snake Mouth, or Shekou, where we arrived at daybreak.

We did not need to move stealthily or make secret signals. The Chinese welcomed smuggled goods; the local authorities supported what we did. People would be waiting for us as we moored. The unloading was fast: a quick cup of tea and we would turn around to row back to Hong Kong. We were paid thirty dollars a trip — not bad money in those days.

No, we weren't much worried by the Hong Kong Marine Police. You see, the whole operation was controlled by former government officials. They had excellent contacts. When we were caught, we were bailed out so fast — the day after our arrest we would be free again. We didn't even have to pay a fine. Everything was arranged for us.

It was a risky business though. We were always afraid of running into pirates who were lying in wait for us at the Green Mountain, or Chingshan, which you know as Castle Peak. They took our steel and sometimes the sampans as well. They were brutal and quite unpredictable. I never knew if I would get away with my life. On one occasion, they beat me, tied me up and left me lying on a beach throughout a long cold night. I was lucky to survive and that somebody found me.

Playing hide-and-seek with pirates had become too dangerous for my liking, so I decided to change my way of life. Some of my fishing friends had already gone ashore and told me stories of life as a coolie. They were working in Yaumatei and I followed them there.

But don't get me wrong, I was never one of those guys you see carrying loads on bamboo poles. We were harbour coolies. We unloaded cargo from boats: rice, firewood, cement. The rice came in heavy bags — ten bags to a ton, each bag weighing 168 catties. We used hooks to move the cargo into huge nets which were then shifted by large cranes. In those days I was tall and strong. I never had any trouble finding work.

In fact our work was well organised. There were coolie-houses where we would all gather. I used to get up very early every morning and arrive at the tea-house about five o'clock, just as it opened. The headman would arrive by six and assign us jobs. 'I want you, you and you,' he would say, pointing.

We would be driven in trucks to Jordan Wharf or to Yaumatei. After work, we would return to the coolie-house to collect our pay. Each of us had been given a little tablet inscribed with the name of the house which we would exchange for cash. We made about five dollars fifty a day; thirty cents of that went to the house.

We worked seven days a week. Sometimes we earned triple wages. We would work until three or four in the morning unloading cargo. It was good money. But if I had worked that hard all the time, my strength would soon have failed me. Sometimes we got a break. One good thing about Hong Kong weather is it rains a lot. When it rained, holds were closed to protect the cargo. We would hole up in the comfortable lounges of the ship, resting or playing thirteen-card Russian poker. Even though we couldn't work, we would be paid our regular wages. So of course, we always prayed for rain.

My family? Yes I had a family. That is where all my money went. That is why I have no savings today. I met my wife when we were both in our thirties. She came from a Yaumatei fishing family. We got married very simply. We didn't have much of a ceremony, we never even got a certificate. We just moved in with each other. Four children were born: three girls and a boy.

At times it was hard to feed them all. After the war rice was still rationed and cost one dollar a catty. That is the equivalent of a hundred dollars a catty today! It was only after the government did away with ration cards that things improved. But all in all, we didn't live badly. I even owned my own boat that was moored in Yaumatei typhoon shelter. Every evening I would pay a sampan to take me home. I never needed to take anything but money back. There were floating shops for everything in Yaumatei. You could buy rice, meat, eggs, beer, sweets — anything you needed for daily living. My wife rarely came ashore; some people living out there never did.

My wife has passed away now. My daughters are all married. My son got an education. He studied at the 'Jesus School' which was run by the Catholics in the typhoon shelter. He did very well and got a job with the Marine Department. Soon he will be a coxswain.

Unfortunately, my daughter-in-law has been causing problems between us. We had all lived together on the junk until the government cleared the Yaumatei shelter and took our boat away. We were not given compensation in cash but allocated a small flat in Wongtaisin housing estate. My son had five children by then. The place wasn't all that crowded; but my daughter-in-law complained a lot and bullied me. She wanted me out. Hell, she kicked me out, the bitch. That is why I am here in this hostel.

Perhaps I should have stayed at sea. But you know — fisherman or coolie — once you are old it's much the same for all of us. Your strength has gone, your body's used up and you are no good to anybody any more. For ordinary working people like myself, life never changes much.

# *Days of the warlords*

**T**his year I shall be seventy-seven. I was a schoolteacher in Chengtu, Szechwan Province, where my married daughter still lives. I couldn't stay with her — there just wasn't room. I have relatives in Taiwan and America, so I came to Hong Kong to see if I could visit them. But it was difficult to get visas and soon my money ran out. So how could I travel abroad?

At that time, I couldn't find anywhere to stay in Hong Kong. Everything here is so expensive. In Chengtu we had problems with housing as well, but the supply of food and consumer goods was quite good. It's a nice place, Chengtu. I lived in Shansi Province during the war, and I can tell you that people in Szechwan were much better off.

During the Cultural Revolution there were some people who wanted to denounce me. They said I had treated a portrait of Chairman Mao with disrespect. But I denied it and after a while they left me alone. Many other teachers, though, had a bad time and were sent down to the countryside. My pupils mostly behaved correctly towards me, but afterwards the schools were closed anyway.

Since I've come to live in this home, things have been quite alright. I can write to my family on the mainland. I have this little room, which I share with another old woman, but I would like to be on my own or with someone else. She cooks in a very smelly way and at night she uses the chamber-pot instead of going out to the toilet. I have asked her to stop but she won't listen. She is in there asleep now, so I just sit in the open air and read my book.

I read a lot — mostly memoirs and reminiscences and autobiographies. Sometimes it is difficult to get the books I want. It costs too much to go down to Kowloon, and anyway the crowds there confuse me. But the warden here is a very good man and sometimes he brings me books. It's not easy to be alone in one's old age. But I don't want to be a burden to my relatives or children. And here I have the company of all kinds of people.

I remember the days of the warlords in Szechwan and Shansi. In Szechwan we had Liu Xiang and Yang Sang. They lived in great luxury and extorted heavy taxes. So most people were destitute by the end of the war. Liu Xiang was an old friend and ally of General Chiang Kai-shek. During the Red Army's Long March — when they were moving northward from the Gold Sand River and entered Szechwan — Chiang Kai-shek cabled Liu Xiang and asked him to stop the Red Bandits, as he called them. That's the story we heard. But the people, especially the local tribes, hated both the warlords and the Kuomintang. The Red Army, led by Lin Piao, got through successfully.

Life was even worse in Shansi. The warlord there, Yen Hsi-shan, was fighting both the Japanese and the Communists at the same time. He was a hard and vicious man. He was so mean — people said he would tax a man's excrement. Later I heard that Yen Hsi-shan had died in Taiwan. I don't know what happened to the others.

The food shortage was terrible in Shansi, so after the war we went back to Chengtu, my husband and I. He died over twenty years ago. I never went back to work after the Cultural Revolution.

*Yip Sik-hong*

Schoolteachers had a very bad time on the whole. So many of them didn't want to work again when Deng Xiao-ping — he is from Szechwan too — had them released and returned to their jobs. His son was badly injured in the Cultural Revolution when the Red Guards pushed him out of a window. Now he is organising relief for the disabled; I think that is very good.

I'm lucky. I have my health, though sometimes of course I feel a bit lonely. I can't afford to buy an aeroplane ticket and in any case it would be awkward living off the charity of relatives. I get a little pocket money sent to me sometimes and it is enough for my small needs. I just really would like to be moved away from this room to be on my own or with someone else.

*Wong Kan-shing*

# I've never gone back

**M**y family were Hakka people from Muiyuen and I was born there in eastern Kwangtung. We were quite well off. My father went to Singapore and worked in a bank there. He sent money back, and the family used it to buy land and hire people to work it. We also got rent for some of it.

My mother stayed on in our village. She had eight children and four of them died. We had a large house; about a hundred of our clansmen lived in it. The Wongs are a big clan and we had a separate ancestral hall. Thousands of us would gather to celebrate the New Year. Yet we lived simply. The Hakka tradition is against any display of wealth. Our clothes were dark and plain, and our women didn't wear the bright red *kwa*. The older ones, who had bound feet, were not carried in sedan-chairs; they had to walk.

The town of Muiyuen was nearby. Chungshan College was there, as well as many middle schools — more than thirty of them — and lots of primary schools. I studied in a middle school for a while. And I was married in my teens. My mother followed the Hakka custom: she took in a young girl, a relative's daughter, and brought her up in our household. We played and studied together until it was time for us to get married.

I was going to join my father in Singapore but my uncle talked me into going to Hong Kong to work for him. I was about twenty-three then and we had four children; but they and my wife stayed behind. My uncle had a small factory in Kowloon, making leather goods like suitcases and handbags. I worked there and also helped to distribute the goods to small shops all over Hong Kong. We sent some goods overseas too.

I've been in Hong Kong for almost fifty years. I was here during the Japanese occupation. All business stopped and we had hardly anything to eat. It cost about four hundred dollars in occupation money for a catty of rice. My uncle had to close his factory and I tried to make a living by selling second-hand clothes. After the war I worked in a small wig factory in Kwuntong. But I was no good at it and had to leave. Then I became a watchman on building sites. When I was sixty-four I fell ill and was taken to hospital. By then I had used up all my savings.

I've been in Helping Hand shelters for five years. The Social Welfare people arranged it; I'd lived in a housing estate before. I'm thankful to be here; I'm comfortable here. I'd like to help others by doing some charitable work, but my health is too poor...

Somehow, I've never been back to China. I know my children are still there but I have no contact with them.

# *In times of great chaos*

**W**hen I was young we lived in Canton in a big house with a courtyard. There were many servants and the household was always bustling with activity. My father was well off — he and his brother-in-law ran two restaurants in Hong Kong. In those days people could pass freely to and fro, and although my father was busy in Hong Kong he came home regularly.

Our family owned two dragon boats and raced them in the Canton Dragon Boat Festival. I remember all the excitement there was. The Dragons were about ninety feet long. There were at least forty men with paddles on each. The heads and tails of the Dragons were painted in blue and gold and so were the enormous drums which were beaten furiously as the boats raced for victory. We'd shout and cheer. What a noisy celebration it was, but what fun!

Yes, I was sent to school. We would go every day, each of us carrying a little desk and stool. But I'm afraid I was rather naughty and often used to skip my lessons. I can read but my writing is not all that it might be.

My mother died when I was nine and I came to live with my aunt in Hong Kong until it was time to return to Canton to get married. The marriage had been arranged when the bridegroom and I were both young children. He came from Fatshan and he was very proud of the fact that he had attended the same school as Dr Sun Yat-sen — Mantak School in Mantak Road. You must have heard of Dr Sun Yat-sen? He was the man who stopped foot-binding and the binding of girls' breasts to make them flat. I did not have my feet bound, nor did my mother, but one of my older sisters did.

My husband and his friends ran a glass factory in Hong Kong. Later they opened another factory in Swatow and that's where our son was born. Then the Japanese war against China began and I returned to Hong Kong with my little son and a maid. My husband couldn't get away. He sent me a letter giving advice on what to do if the war grew any worse. He wrote: 'In times of great chaos one should live in the countryside; in times of minor unrest one should live in the town.'

I thought this over and decided to leave Hong Kong to go back to live in Fatshan. But we were cheated and robbed so shamelessly by the people there that we returned to Hong Kong. Eventually I rejoined my husband in Swatow. It was then about 1938 and the Japanese were coming close. They bombed our factory and, although the damage was not serious, we felt it was time to get out. So we left with a few servants and some of our belongings and made what turned out to be a long trip in search of safety. First we travelled across to Kweilin, in Kwangsi Province; and from there we went on all the way up to Chungking in Szechwan.

It was a mountainous journey and I was terribly scared when the rough road took us along the heights with a sheer drop on one side. Some of the time I travelled in a sedan-chair and sometimes I walked. My little boy was six. He would walk part of the way and then be carried. At times the going was very rough, deep in mud. There were many people on the move fleeing the Japanese. But at least we had no trouble from bandits. We would stay overnight in peasants' huts in the villages. They would charge us a few coins. In the end we settled in a village some distance from

*Yuen Yin-ping*

Chungking. We escaped the bombing of the city. When the war was all over we returned to Swatow.

After the Communists took over in China my life changed completely. My husband and I came to live in Hong Kong with our son. But soon after 1949 my son, with other students, returned to the mainland for a university course in engineering. We had one letter from him and that was all. No more news, no more contact. I have never discovered what became of him.

After my husband died I went to stay with another branch of our family. But even though it was family I was harassed and abused. This made me ill and depressed and I was admitted to hospital. Later a hospital official referred me to this home — where, at last, I can live in peace.

# *Once a General*

**W**hen I was young I was full of hope and ideals. Like many other students of my generation I wanted to work for China and the betterment of our people. I wanted to make our country count again and see our nation prosper.

Now that I am old I feel nothing but shame. I did not serve my people well. I did not help them towards a better future. My contributions were minor and few; and whatever I did was wasted in the end. Because of my failures and those of others like me, my fellow citizens on the mainland are still suffering — their fate has been to 'fall into deep water and huge flames'.

I was born in 1912 in Hunan Province. I knew Mao Tse-tung when I was a boy. My oldest brother had been a schoolmate of his at Changsha and I saw him on many occasions. In those days he was beginning to study Marxist thinking. He was never a good person — even when young!

My own student days were spent at Nanking University where I studied agriculture. However, I never graduated. Because the country was at war, I left university and joined the Military Academy at Changsha. I spent almost thirteen years in the army, about eight of them on or near the front. My last rank was that of major-general in the Kuomintang army.

Yes, I've seen a lot of action. I served with the New First Army fighting the Japanese; to start with in China, then in Burma. Later I was in India where I was attached to the Allies as an observer. Likewise, American and other military advisers were attached to our forces. Of course, before World War II, we had German instructors at the military schools as well. But Germany conspired with the Japanese against us. America sold us out at Yalta. And Russia, pretending to be friendly with Chiang Kai-shek, was all the time secretly propping up the Chinese Communist Party, turning its members into traitors and criminals.

When World War II ended, I was ordered by the KMT command to the northwest of China to fight against the Red Army. But the Communists already occupied most of the mainland — their agents were everywhere. The population, exhausted by war and famine, was easily deceived by their smiles and promises. The defeat of the Kuomintang was not a military one. The Communists won the people.

You talk about corruption within the KMT; but can you honestly claim that there is no corruption within the Communist Party? There is an old saying: 'Large trees have withered branches.' It is not surprising that the Chinese nation produces a lot of 'bad people' as there are so many of us and the general level of civilisation and education is very low. Of course, it is often unavoidable that a retreating army creates chaos in the countryside. But in regular military fighting units, such as mine, discipline remained strict and the soldiers behaved well.

In 1946 I was posted to a military training base in Taiwan. I held the post of a chief staff officer. At that time my monthly salary was seventeen thousand new Taiwan yuan. My life was very comfortable then.

By 1948 the military situation on the mainland had become confused. The Kuomintang was

*Yeung Po*

negotiating with the Communists in Nanking. As there was an acute shortage of officers in Taiwan, I was posted back to the mainland to recruit trainees. In 1949 I reached Kwangtung and later the same year I left for Hunan. But it was all too late. The Communists seized the whole of China and I was trapped on the mainland.

Over the next two years I waged guerrilla warfare against the Communists. I was the leader of a group of more than seven hundred men. We hid in the mountains, waiting to ambush the soldiers of the People's Army. But it was hopeless. Many men deserted. The Reds began hunting for me and in the end I decided to escape. I walked, climbing the hills, then finally reached a town where I took a train to the border station at Lowu.

Once in Hong Kong I informed the KMT military command about my escape. But as I had previously had many disagreements with my commanding officers, I decided not to return to Taiwan and to leave the army.

At first I found work in the editorial department of the Hong Kong Times, a Kuomintang paper. I wrote about military history, Chinese and international. However, it was difficult to find research material in Hong Kong. And because I am a military man and not a literary person, I also found it difficult to get along with my colleagues. In the end, I left the paper to go into business.

I had very little money of my own. But, through family connections, I was able to raise enough capital to get off to a good start. First I owned a knitting factory. Later, I opened a grocery shop, the Wah Hing store on Gloucester Road, and for a while all went well. I made some money, travelled, and even married again. But in the end, because of my lack of business experience, my companies failed. I went broke and lost everything.

You want to know about my wives? I was married three times. My first wife was shot by the Communists. My second wife and three children stayed behind in Hunan when I left. I have always assumed that she was killed as well; but in truth, I don't really know what became of her or my children. After I left China I wasn't able to write to them. Had any relatives received letters from me, they would have been accused of 'counter-revolutionary activities'. Much later, when the political tensions had eased, I was unable to locate them.

I met my third wife on a visit to Germany during the early Fifties. I had been invited there by one of my former teachers; there were family business connections as well. I stayed in Hamburg for several weeks. It was there that I met my American-Jewish wife. Now this may sound very strange to you: a Jewish girl in Germany falling in love with a Chinese nationalist. But such things happen. After all, didn't President Chiang Ching-kuo in Taiwan bring home a Russian bride? There was deep feeling between us and we loved each other.

We were married in New York City in 1953. My wife's family was in the diamond business and well-to-do. After the wedding we remained in the States for three months and then moved back to Hong Kong. We lived in Happy Valley and later in Kowloon. My wife studied Chinese and helped in the store. We had three children.

Then, well over twenty years ago, when my wife and I were on a sightseeing tour in Denmark, we had a car crash and my wife was killed. The shock was terrible. I didn't know what to do. Financially, I was already going downhill. My business was failing. I had little time for my children and they missed their mother. In the end, I handed them over to their maternal grandmother in New York. There was money there and they would receive a better education. I returned, alone, to Hong Kong.

In the beginning I communicated regularly with my children. Then their grandmother passed away and letters arrived less frequently. It was largely my fault. I had lost my business and was fast becoming a pauper. I was ashamed and did not want my children to learn of my poverty. For long periods, I didn't have a regular address. Finally we lost touch completely. Some time ago I did go to the American Consulate to ask for help; but they were unable to locate my family for me.

After the collapse of my business, I tried my hand at various jobs. First, I thought I might find work as a writer again. But to find employment in the literary world of Hong Kong, you need to have connections. You need to bow and kowtow.

Finally, I became a hawker. I peddled fruit on the streets of Kowloon. But this work too I had to give up as I could not afford a licence and was harassed by triads and police. Every day thugs from the triads would come and extort thirty dollars from me. If I refused to hand over the money, they would beat me up or tell the police to arrest me. Hong Kong society is like that — even now. I don't want to talk about it any more!

So you wonder why I haven't returned to Taiwan? It's a matter of self-respect. In the past I was an officer of high rank. Now, all my former junior officers hold high positions in Taiwan while I have become a nobody. It would be difficult for me to face them. Once or twice in the past, it is true, I have visited Taiwan. My former comrades were most respectful and urged me to apply for a government pension. But I always refused as I did not want to add to the burden of my country. After all, to serve one's country and one's government is the duty of every citizen.

# *Born to sing*

**I** was born to be a singer. I was born to be a star. Nearly all my life I've been an entertainer and, although I'm now sixty-seven, I'm still ready to sing Cantonese opera any time anybody asks me. And I can still dance. At the International Hotel in Macau in the old days I was the lead dancer. Waltz, tango, foxtrot — I enjoyed them all. I was the one who taught the new girls. One step here, one step there, swing — and round and round again. Sometimes we would perform on stage, sometimes we joined patrons on the dance floor. I won much acclaim. Those were my golden days.

When I was young I lived in a farmhouse in Kwangtung Province, the daughter of a second wife. That is her picture, on the table there. She was wonderful to me. Nobody had such a mother! She worked as a dressmaker and put money aside to send me to kindergarten and primary school. Then, when I was about ten years old, we moved to Macau where work was easier to come by. I continued my schooling, studying the Chinese classics and a bit of English. I worked hard and my mother was well pleased with me.

It was really just by chance that I happened to become a professional singer. I had this girl friend in Macau. She lived next door to us and was the daughter of a woman hawker who sold salt-fish at the roadside. Well, my girl friend belonged to a singing group and one day she asked me to go along with her and she introduced me to her teacher. He was a kind and gifted man. He saw right away that I had talent and potential and he invited me to become his student. I spent ten years with him learning how to cultivate my voice and perform on stage. He taught me how to sing in the various styles of Cantonese opera: male or female voice — high, low or medium. I learned how to move on stage and how every step and gesture has its own significance. I learned how to fight with swords and how to tumble like an acrobat. I studied many plays and many parts.

No, I never had to pay for tuition. It wasn't done like that. You simply offered presents at important festivals. But sometimes, when I was still training, my teacher would send me on an engagement. Then my fee would be three patacas — that's three dollars — for two songs. I'll sing for you now if you like, and I can play on my *tsin-tsin* which I've still got on the wall here. Yes, I suppose it does look a bit like a mandolin . . .

Well, after I'd worked at the International Hotel in Macau I moved on to the Central Hotel. We always used a very good Shanghai tailor — they are the best you know — to make our cheongsams, following fashion as it moved from high collar to low or from long skirt to short. I also wore western-style evening gowns and developed a good eye for choosing what suited me. In my free time I kept fit with bicycle riding and roller-skating. Those were happy days. I was living with my mother and we were comfortably off.

Marriage? No, I never married legally. Most men are not reliable. I had some good times, mind you, but I never went in for anything permanent. So I never had children. I've had some sour feelings about that but, you know, my mother was a Buddhist and I have learned something from her — to accept God's will as controlling our destiny.

*Tong Siu-wah*

Oh, so you know about the Black Society, the triad gangs with their protection rackets that get hold of girls in dancing places? Well, I tell you now, they never got hold of me. I was a star and I never let them come anywhere near me. Of course, in those early days, the Black Society was not nearly such a serious problem as it became later.

After the war, life was never quite the same in Macau. Sometime, in the early Sixties, the gambling concession changed hands and as a result the Central Hotel was closed down. The entertainment business suffered badly. Of course, I have to admit, I was getting on a bit and in my profession there's always the likelihood of a new queen coming along. In any case, engagements became rare.

Finally my mother and I moved to Hong Kong and I found work washing dishes in a restaurant. My mother died in 1977 at the age of ninety-four. As I myself have neither son nor daughter I consider myself lucky to have been introduced to this home. But I still like to sing. And I can still dance. Stay a little longer — let me show you the steps of the slow foxtrot. Alright then, perhaps next time. You know, the Autumn Festival will be here in a few days. And I've been asked to sing at the concert they are organising here. I'm really looking forward to it.

# *The Great Storm*

I was raised as a child on our family junk and one of the earliest things I can remember is the Great Storm. There was no early warning in those days — I'm talking about more than seventy-five years ago. The sky darkened suddenly and the wind rose — a westerly wind, a killing wind — and all the junks in the harbour were blown towards Causeway Bay. Many sank on the way.

It was an eerie sight: the harbour empty of ships because they had all been driven eastwards. But there were many people clinging to floating wreckage — calling out, drowning. Our own junk was driven against a pier on the Hong Kong side of the harbour. My uncle grabbed me in his arms and flung me to safety. I was very young and just ran; I was terrified. Later I came back to the pier and there was nothing there — no boat, nothing. Men with handcarts were taking away the dead. Later I found my family alive; but the junk was gone for ever.

Although we had spent most of our time on the junk, we had a cubicle in Kowloon rented from friends in a four storey tenement house in Temple Street. You know those cubicles: ours was a middle one, without windows, dark all day; you had to use oil lamps. That was our place ashore; so we stayed there after the junk went down.

I learned later that up to then we hadn't been doing badly, carrying cases of cloth from Kowloon side to the big ocean-going ships out in the harbour. Besides my father and mother there were an uncle and brothers and an older sister. We children had no schooling: as soon as we were able to, we worked all day with the grown-ups, humping those cases of cloth. Sometimes, if there was a slack hour or so, we might play in the water around our boat; but we didn't have time for games with children from other families.

For us boys, the best time of the year was at the Tin Hau Festival. As you know, Tin Hau is the patron goddess of all us boat-dwellers and fishing folk. She has many temples all over Hong Kong where we pray for protection from bad winds and seas and ask her help for good fishing. There were shrines on the junks as well, where we burned joss-sticks and made offerings.

The birthday of Tin Hau is celebrated every year on the twenty-third day of the third moon. I always got very excited as the day drew near. My mother would go shopping ashore which was most unusual; normally she'd buy all our food from the sampan-shops. My father bought strings of red-packet firecrackers and we boys would put up the banners with which all junks were decorated. Just in front of the mast we would have a big screen wishing the goddess a 'happy birthday'. There would be many signal flags, with large triangular banners in green or yellow behind the mast. On the after-deck would be lanterns and shrines to Tin Hau together with our offerings.

On the day of the celebration our junk would set out for the temple in Joss House Bay, which is believed to be the most important temple of the goddess. If the weather was against us we would be towed by tugs — but otherwise we would sail, the banners fluttering in the wind. When we arrived there would be a terrible scramble as everybody wanted to be the first ashore and up the hill. Then we'd carry the shrines to the temple and present our offerings. Yes, those were happy

*Cheng Yung*

days and Tin Hau was greatly honoured on those occasions. But in the year of the Great Storm we must have angered her; she failed to look after us.

We lost a lot of cargo in that typhoon and there was no insurance. But my parents somehow got another junk. I remember one job we did — carrying big stones and boulders from Cheung Chau island for the building of the Yaumatei typhoon shelter. We were subcontractors to a firm called Sun Lee and were paid by the ton; it worked out at about ten dollars for a full load.

Our junk had no engine. If the wind was in our favour we could make the run from Cheung Chau to the harbour in one or two hours and then ten dollars was a good rate. If the wind was against us it was terribly hard work and not to be compared with the five dollars per cargo from shore to ship in Central. We always had enough to eat though. In those days, before World War I, a plate of noodles cost you only two or three cents.

I was married when I was nineteen. A relative acted as matchmaker and my bride was a girl who worked on the barges in Macau. Of our four children two died very young; but I still have a daughter and six grandsons — all living on Peng Chau island. The youngest is twelve.

During the Japanese occupation I continued working on the junk. The Japanese paid me forty catties of rice per cargo. My last surviving son died soon after the war, and I kept working the junk with paid help, but when my wife died I gave it up and went to sell fish in Tsuenwan market. Later I went line-fishing. It didn't pay too badly; you got twenty dollars a catty for garoupa.

Until recently I lived alone in a wooden hut on Tsing Yi Island. When the government knocked it down under a clearance scheme, I came here to Lai King Shelter. I share my room with another chap and do his cooking for him. In the evening we eat early and watch TV. I have few worries now. Tin Hau is protecting me.

# My daughter was gone

**M**y name is Wong Hing-ki. I was born in 1903 in Siuhing, which is way to the west of Canton. I was named Hing after my birthplace. My father owned a shop that sold wedding items — bedding, wedding tents, cake-boxes, couplets and so on. When I was small I lived at the back of the store, but as our family grew, my father built a new house. It was there, a few lanes behind the store, that I grew up happily with my two brothers and four sisters.

I had no formal education. Both my brothers were instructed in the classics by a hired tutor. Even after they were married and had children they continued their studies. But not us girls. In those days learning was not considered suitable or necessary for women. But I am not totally uneducated. I learned to identify Chinese characters by cutting them out to paste onto cloth or paper to make wedding couplets. If their meaning was not explained to me, I would refuse to cut the characters. Sometimes I would trace them with ink. Even now, I can still read a little.

I was married when I was about seventeen. As was customary, it was a blind marriage arranged by a marriage-broker. But times were bad in the country. There was civil war and when we tried to escape the fighting I lost both my husband and my little son. That's why I had to bring up my daughter all by myself. I would carry her strapped to my back while I made a living weaving towels. Then there was no more cotton and I had to take odd jobs to make ends meet. My baby was always with me.

When my daughter was a bit older I found work as a domestic servant with a gentleman. It turned out that the gentleman was keeping a mistress, and he was looking for a maid to serve her. She wasn't official, like a concubine, but she was a very nice person and she was very good to me. When I presented my daughter to pay her respects, she was so taken by her that she insisted that I keep her with me in the house. So my daughter joined the household and shared my bed. Unfortunately, only about a year later, the gentleman's wife found out about her husband's affair and arrived to break up the household. You should have heard the noise and fuss she made. She shrieked — you could hear it a mile off! She took away the furniture and just about everything there was in the house. Luckily we had been given some warning and I was able to help my lady take her jewellery and hide it in a safe place before the wife arrived. But I lost my job and a home where we had been happy.

Well, there was nothing for it. I had to find work so that we could eat, so I set out to find another job, which was difficult as people didn't want the extra burden of feeding the two of us. My daughter was a very cute and clever girl. Many times I was asked whether I wanted to sell her or give her away for adoption. But I loved her. I refused to give her up. Finally I found an employer who had four children and allowed me to bring her along. But then, a few years later, the Japanese came. My boss decided he'd move his family to Hong Kong, but he said I couldn't bring my daughter. She was eleven then and had been accepted by a proper school. I didn't know what to do. I lay awake for many sleepless nights. In the end I decided it would be best if I left my daughter behind. I could not allow both of us to die for lack of money and food.

Wong Hing-ki

I took an advance from my employers and gave the money to some relatives to feed and lodge my daughter. But times were bad. Everybody was hungry and looked out for themselves first. My relatives didn't give any money to my daughter and nearly starved her. When I found out, I had no choice but to send for her, and she joined me in Hong Kong. As she couldn't stay with me I boarded her with a family, which cost me five dollars a month. I sold all my wedding jewellery. Those were sad days; life was very difficult. A year later my boss — who had military connections — learned in advance that the Japanese were about to invade Hong Kong. He decided to move his family back to China, but I didn't go because he wouldn't let me take my daughter with me.

The Japanese came and it was hard to find work. I sold peanuts for a while but didn't earn enough to live on. Then I went into the hills and collected rice which I sold in Western District on the streets. One day I was robbed. Three men came and accused me of not using a correct scale. They became fierce, pushed me over, and ran off with everything I had.

Anyway, in order to survive I took the lowliest of all jobs. I became a night-soil collector. Even when times were hard in China I would never have dreamed of taking on filthy, degrading work like that. But I had to feed my daughter, and I was willing to do anything for her. It was horrible. They put newcomers to work in the very old buildings — up and down flights of broken and narrow staircases and up onto the rooftops. The buckets were heavy and full almost to the top. We started to collect this horrible stuff at about one in the morning. The older workers rushed us and yelled at us all the time. I felt so humiliated and frustrated. I only lasted six months in that job.

Then I decided to have my daughter come and live with me. It was better to stay together, I felt, even though we'd only have *congee* to eat. I rented a bed-space in Temple Street. The front room was occupied by a couple and their granddaughter; the middle room belonged to a man who was never there. I rented the back room which, because of poor ventilation, was much cheaper and cost me only fifty cents a month.

In those days they were hiring labour at the airport. The foreman was a young man of about thirty who worked for the Labour Union organised by the Japanese. I was almost forty and I knew how to handle this foreman. The pay was forty cents a day and a catty of rice. I agreed to take only twelve liang, or three-quarters of the rice, with the rest going to the foreman. So, of course, I got the job. We carried bricks, moved planks of wood and helped demolish buildings to make room for the airport. During our lunch break, at noon, the foreman would line up all the women workers and get us to sit down on benches and chatter, tell stories and sing songs — because the Japanese usually came by at that time. Two women would be on watch and when the Japanese soldiers approached we would clap our hands to welcome them.

Then, one day, I heard that another unit at the airport was hiring labourers to work at night. The pay was better — one dollar, with more rice as well. The shift began at six in the evening and lasted till five in the morning, with time for a short midnight snack. We'd huddle around a charcoal fire, put some rice in a tin cup, add water and some tiny saltfish to it and enjoy our break.

I was very happy to have so much rice, which was hard to come by those days. My daughter too was beginning to put some flesh on her bones and her cheeks were a healthy pink. We were together and content.

I worked very hard. Then, one morning, I came home and my daughter was gone. She had disappeared! She simply wasn't there. My neighbours told me she had carried some bedding with her when she left — nothing else, not even rice. She had seemed in a hurry, they said, and perhaps she was scared. But she hadn't said anything, nor left word. Nobody knew where she'd gone or why — but, of course, there was talk and we had our suspicions. In those days the Japanese were rounding up people all over town, as they thought the population of Hong Kong was too large to feed. And they sent all those people to Lantau Island, where they would starve but no one would be around to notice it. You don't believe me? But this is what everybody said was happening. And it is true that all the time they were rounding up people — and those people were never seen again. So you can see why I couldn't ask the Japanese about my daughter. All they would have done was to send me to Lantau as well. And, of course, I couldn't be sure that she wouldn't come back. But she never did. I kept hoping. I went to the temple and prayed. But I never saw her again.

I became ill. I felt worse every day. One morning I woke up and saw a lot of people around my bed, but I couldn't hear a sound. A neighbour sent for a doctor who gave me some injections that probably saved my life. But I lost all hearing in one of my ears. As I was not well enough to work I decided to go back to my native village to rest until I got better. I stayed there during the last part of the war. Then, one day, a neighbour came rushing in. She told me that firecrackers were sounding off everywhere and that peace had been proclaimed. I was both happy and sad. The war was over, but my daughter had not come back to me.

I knew I couldn't stay at my father's house forever. But where was I to go and what was I to do? Finally a relative introduced me to a fine old woman who said I could work for her godson in Canton. So I went down to Canton to work for a family called Sun. To begin with all went well. But soon, due to inflation, I found my wages were worth less and less until I hardly earned enough to buy a pair of wooden clogs. The Suns could not afford to keep me under those circumstances and so I came back to Hong Kong again and worked in domestic jobs here for several years.

In 1965 I was told that a plastics factory was hiring. There was a fat man who was the factory manager. He looked at me coldly and asked me whether I was seeking a job for my daughter or granddaughter. When I told him I was looking for myself he said I was too old to be hired. I was very disappointed. I was only sixty-two. How was I going to live if I was too old for work? Then I had a stroke of luck. A woman I'd met when I joined the Catholic Church told me she knew the boss of that factory. She said she could help me get the job — and she did.

I worked in the factory making plastic flowers until the 1967 riots. There was a lot of unrest in Hong Kong then and one morning I was going to work on a tram when there was a bomb scare.

The tram stopped near Shaukeiwan and I had to walk all the way to the factory in North Point. By the time I arrived the gates were already closed. They wouldn't let me in. I was given the wages owed to me and dismissed. I thought this was very unfair.

But I won't bore you any more with talk about all the odd jobs I did after that. I managed to feed myself until 1976 and then I applied for Public Assistance. At that time I was living in a very crowded place — what we call a sausage room, which was shared by three different parties. The room was six feet long but very narrow. The three beds were one on top of the other and there was barely any space to walk in. Of course, it was cheap. The rent was only twenty-four dollars a month and we each paid eight dollars. Over the years the price went up but I stayed there until 1985. Then I went to the District Office and they sent me to Helping Hand.

Yes, I am very comfortable here. They've told me that I can now apply for a flat of my own in one of those big government buildings. But how would I survive there without a family to care for me? You see, in the mornings now, I don't remember what happened last night. Nor do I know what the evening may bring. At my age, and I'm eighty-five, I appreciate receiving attention and living in a community. It would all be so different if my daughter had come back.

# *A triad life*

廖
華
宗

**I** have never misbehaved or bullied people. However, if you were to hit me once, I would hit you back three times. If you were to push me to the extent that I have to raise my hand, there would be no place for you to hide — not even under your mother's pants. That is my philosophy of life.

No, I don't look Chinese. My father's mother was Malay and I was born in Singapore. My grandfather was Chinese though, and when I was ten I was sent back to our native village in China to study at the village school. Our family were Hakkas. They made their living from farming and I helped them. I did not finish school.

When I was about sixteen I joined the Kuomintang army. I was a soldier for almost ten years and at one point commanded several thousand men. Now that I'm sixty-four you may find this difficult to believe, but then I was young and strong and learning fast. If somebody would not obey me, I would beat him into submission. I would hit first, before talking and explaining — that is why I was put in charge. We went all over China. In Hunan we fought the Japanese but I never fought against the Communists.

I ran away from the KMT because everybody was corrupt, especially the top officials. Because they were corrupt they could not rule the people and the soldiers would not obey them. You see, all the army was paid for and provisioned by the Americans. Top officers would get paid in American dollars while the lower ranks and common soldiers received worthless 'military currency'. Officers wore rich clothes and ate well. The soldiers wore 'mosquito net' — tattered clothing — and were forced to steal from the people. They took pigs, chickens, dogs and rice — anything for food. I have seen rape and worse. The soldiers did terrible things to people.

I left China in 1948 when the Chinese Communist Party was taking over. Otherwise, as a former KMT soldier, I might have been shot. Many of my friends were. Ten of my buddies escaped from a Communist jail and tried to make their way to Hong Kong. On the border the guards shot two of them and two others drowned trying to swim to Hong Kong. I lost touch with the survivors but I have heard that some emigrated to America.

When I first came to Hong Kong I made my money by stealing. Yes, I robbed homes. I took money and pawned the valuables. I was caught by the police many times; each time they put me in prison for a few months. Once I was sent to Stanley prison for several years because I had resisted arrest. In those days the police were very corrupt. There was no lawyer to defend me and the police did whatever they wanted with the likes of us.

I might as well tell you now. I met up with my triad brothers soon after I arrived in Hong Kong. Many of us in the KMT army belonged to the 14K gang. I joined the triads when I was in Canton because my Commander introduced me. He became my 'big brother' — we shared the same surname. After the war he had settled in Macau, from where he commanded many ex-KMT soldiers, all members of the 14K. In those days you couldn't get along without joining. And once you've joined, there's no escape. Even if you don't look for them, they'll come looking for you!

*Liu Wah-chung*

They used to assign ten members to a 'territory' — usually an area you knew well. But because of my previous high standing in the 14K, I was allowed to move on and work the territories that were most profitable. I was supposed to split profits — sixty per cent to me and forty per cent to them; but I never gave them their proper share and I got away with it. You've got to be smart and respected to survive; but, as I said before, I had good standing and protection.

You don't earn a salary as a triad member; making a living depends on how smart you are. Even now I don't need to pay for my cigarettes. The way you walk when you approach a cigarette stall — they know immediately you are a member of a gang and they will give you cigarettes for free. I retired from the 14K after my 'big brother' died — the one who introduced me to the gang in Canton. He passed away about seven years ago. Since then I've had little contact with the gang.

I never saved any money. When I had any I gambled it away. I regret that very much now. Of course, one other reason for always being poor was because I smoked opium. You see I used to smoke a lot — five to six cups a time. A friend introduced me to it, shortly after I arrived in Hong Kong. The first time I smoked I was sick for three days. I hit my friend for giving it to me. Then I became an addict myself.

You want to know about my family? I had been married for over a year when I first came to Hong Kong. We had one daughter. She and my wife are still in China. I have not heard from them for twenty years now. I would very much like to go and visit them in Canton but I don't have the money to make the trip.

I didn't always earn my living stealing. At one time I got a job in a textile factory and learned how to work with machines. It was a skilled job and I made nine hundred to one thousand dollars a month, which wasn't bad pay in those days. Later I became a construction worker, painting and plastering, and was getting fifty to sixty dollars a day.

When I was in my fifties I became a hawker, selling food. I had to borrow money from friends to start the business. Even now, I still owe a few thousand dollars. I am paying it back from my Public Assistance at thirty to forty dollars a month. I never got a hawking licence, which costs seven to eight thousand dollars. Every time I was caught I paid the five hundred dollars penalty and also had the food I was selling confiscated. You see, it's hard to live straight.

# *A gang of girls*

**M**y family comes from Namhoi County. I was born in 1913 in Canton, where my father owned a shoe shop. My mother had thirteen children — nine girls and four boys — but many of them died young. One brother drowned as a child. Another was kidnapped. My two other brothers disappeared during the Japanese war. They left the house one morning and never came back. My two elder sisters died as children. I was the eldest girl to survive.

My parents were both uneducated. My mother never learned to read or write and my father was only just literate. When I was small, my mother refused to let me go to school. She said that what had been good enough for her was good enough for me and that girls didn't need a fancy education. But times change and when I was fifteen my father allowed me and my younger sister to attend school. I studied for four years. When I left I could read a newspaper, had lots of good friends, and knew my way around.

We had such fun when I was at school. We were a gang of girls — what you would call teenagers nowadays — and we would get up to all sorts of mischief. Cutting lessons, meeting boys, even smoking! When I was sixteen or seventeen we used to ask our teacher to let us off on Saturdays. We wouldn't tell our parents, who thought we were studying all day. We'd buy ourselves a picnic lunch and sneak off to parks and beauty spots around town. Sometimes we'd meet some boys and go hiking together. Our favourite place was Sha Ho, which is famous for its flat noodles even now.

After I left school I went back to help my mother at home. But I had tasted the free life and continued to go out with my friends and sometimes with boys. My mother disapproved and scolded me. She'd say: 'You're a girl from a well-regarded family. You shouldn't run around with boys. What will people think? Who will want to marry you?' But I didn't care. I had met my future husband by then and we were courting. We'd eat in western-type restaurants using knives and forks. We'd go to nightclubs and western movie shows. Sometimes they didn't finish until after eleven o'clock and I'd get home very late. My father would ask 'Where is everyone?' But my mother was afraid of him and didn't tell him. She would put my slippers outside my room and pretend I was at home and asleep. When I got back I'd wash my face quietly and sneak into bed.

I had known my husband for two years when we decided to get married. He was attending school in Canton at that time. His father owned land in the country and sent his sons to town to improve themselves. Although it was not an arranged marriage, neither of our parents objected. It was agreed that I would go without a dowry and that the wedding would be simple. We arranged a wedding banquet — four tables — for relatives from both families. I wore the red wedding gown, served tea to my parents-in-law and followed the rituals.

After we were married my husband and I went back to his parents' home in the countryside. My husband was the son of the principal wife but, as she had already died, we lived with my second mother-in-law. The family was well-to-do so I didn't have to do any work in the house or fields. At first we were all content. Then, as I was unable to conceive, sadness came into our lives.

*Chow Siu-wan*

You know how it was in those days — you didn't go to the doctor very often and you'd try to cure illness with old-fashioned remedies. Well, I'd had trouble with my menstruation at one point and someone had suggested a certain medicine. It turned out that this had made me sterile. No matter where we went, no matter which doctor we saw nor whose advice we sought, I could not have children. My husband was most upset. He asked me to let him take a concubine, but I refused. I said because there was a war and because times were uncertain it would be unwise to bring another person into the house. My husband understood that my attitude was reasonable.

During the war the family separated and moved all over the place to avoid the Japanese soldiers. My mother-in-law followed her daughter into the interior. My husband — he was about thirty — joined the anti-Japanese forces. I ran away with friends. We went all over Kwangtung Province. After the war I returned to the village. My husband was back, my mother-in-law was back and the land was still there. But we didn't stay for long. The Communists were advancing and there were bad rumours about what happened to landlords in what were known as liberated areas. Before the Red soldiers came to our village we took whatever money we had and ran for Hong Kong. A year later the border was closed.

In Hong Kong my husband tried his hand at various small enterprises — a coffee shop at one point — but none was very successful. We moved a lot; rents were high and we were eventually reduced to living in two rooms. Then my husband had a stroke. He was half paralysed after that. He died in 1972 when he was sixty-six. After my husband's death I was quite poor. I rented a room in Mongkok and sold *dim-sum* in a tea-house. The wage was low but my food was free. Four years ago I applied for Public Assistance and moved into this home. I'm seventy-six and my lifestyle is very modest now. But I'm not uncomfortable and I don't complain.

You know, if I really wanted it, my life could be much improved. My younger sister lives in Hong Kong and her family is quite well-off. When my husband died my sister said 'Come and stay with me' and 'Come and eat with us if you need to'. But you know how difficult family relationships can be. My husband and I were not really well educated and we never learned to speak English. My sister's husband, on the other hand, had gone to university and was an architect in Hong Kong. My sister offers me great kindness but our worlds have grown apart and our meetings are awkward. Under such circumstances it would be wrong to impose.

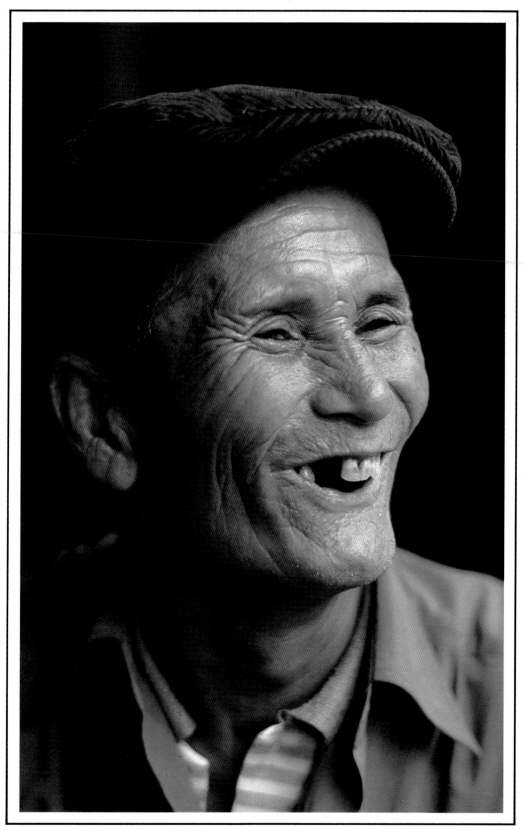

*Wong Wing-kan*

# *Chasing the dragon*

**S**o they told you I'm on methadone. Well, take a good look at me. I'm seventy-five this year and I've never been ill in my life. Not a single day! People say I don't look like a drug addict. I don't look like somebody who eats 'white powder', but I have been on drugs since I first came to Hong Kong.

My name is Wong Wing-kan. I am a native of Shuntak. My parents died when I was very young and my sister and I were raised by an uncle in Mankingsha. My uncles were fishermen and tenant farmers and I helped them when I was a boy. Later, my older sister married into a Macau fishing family and I followed her. I worked as a fisherman — well, to tell you the truth I smuggled goods. I worked for somebody else. That's all I can really tell you.

When the Japanese came, we were all separated. I had to look after myself but I was old enough to know what to do. No, I never was really much bothered by the Japanese soldiers. They were just like anybody else in authority; walking big and giving orders. I can't remember much about them. After all, I was young and mostly interested in having a good time.

I came to Hong Kong shortly before the Communists took over in China in 1949. I had no training and no education so I worked as a coolie. Whenever anyone wanted a job done, I would do it. I made only a few dollars a day to start with, but later I earned more when I worked for a rattan shop in Kowloon near Waterloo Road. Perhaps you have been there?

I have always worked hard because of my drug-taking. As you must surely know, most coolies smoke heroin. Of course, we all started with opium. I never thought of it as something bad or dangerous. All the people I worked with smoked. They would say 'Come now, let's have a smoke'. I was only concerned with having a good time; and then it was too late — I was an addict.

In those days, opium smoking was not forbidden and it was very cheap. The cigarette vendor in the street would sell you a packet, twenty-five cents a go. Later opium became illegal and the price went up. Of course, the police were part of it. They knew all about us. The policemen with the 'flower' — you know, the inspectors with the pip on their shoulders — would walk by and laugh. It was alright to buy then. Later, after the big Kowloon City disturbances, there was a clamp-down on opium. I can't remember the year but it was about the time when ID cards came in. I had no education, I can only relate things to big events.

In any case, when opium became hard to get, we all switched to heroin. I don't know about injecting the 'white powder'. I only 'chased the dragon' — that is, inhaled it. I would put the heroin on foil, then light it — usually in a pipe — and inhale it. You feel wonderful — full of energy! However hard you have to work, you can do it! You know, very few people actually stop working because of being addicted. You have to work to make money for the next smoke. And if you don't work you can't smoke. That's what being an addict is all about.

Of course, I was always short of money. Everything I ever made disappeared into my pipe. Smoking came first. At one period, as soon as I got up in the morning, I had to take at least fifty dollars worth of heroin to get going. If I was offered a job before I had a smoke, I would have to take money on credit, have a smoke and then go to work. Because I was known as a reliable worker, people trusted me and paid me in advance.

When I was about seventy I got to know the owner of a wholesale food-chain. He gave me a job. I started at 3.30 am and would work in the food market until about 7.00 am. After that, the traffic regulations would come into effect and the trucks would not be allowed to stop. I would hang about and do odd jobs for anybody who needed a hand.

In 1981 I was in a motor accident. A car ran into me. I had to have one leg amputated and am now a cripple. I was in hospital for many months. They fitted me with a false leg just before I left. Now, I can't even carry a ten-catty pack of rice. When I was in hospital I was taken off heroin. I was put on methadone instead. I take a dose once every day. I take it because without it I can't sleep and I have heart palpitations. I am given the bus fare and go every day to get my dose. I am examined regularly to see if I am keeping up with the treatment. If I stop, I won't get it any more. Then I won't sleep. So I can't stop.

I never married. I was only concerned with making a living. During the day, I would work hard. In the evening, I would enjoy myself with friends, gambling and smoking. I never had a home. I slept around the places I worked and I would eat at tea-houses or at street stalls. In the winter, friends gave me warm clothing.

Now, my life is very different. I am looked after and pass each day as it comes. If I have extra money I spend it on more food. Sometimes people give me presents. Sometimes when it is stormy, and my leg is painful, the warden buys food for me. I watch television every day. During festivals I watch people being happy.

# *First Class to London*

**I** come from a family of farmers. We lived a few miles north of Shumchun in Po On County, just across the border from Hong Kong. I was born in 1916, the eldest of three girls, and we had a brother who was sixteen years younger than me. Our grandparents lived not far away. Life was hard, but we were a happy and united family. We owned a small piece of land and then there was another piece that we rented. We hired an ox for ploughing, and most of our crops went to the landlord as rent. But he was a fair man. If the harvest failed he would let us put off the rent, or he'd even reduce it if times were really bad.

We were happy because our parents were so good to us. Our father had three years' schooling and learned about the teachings of Confucius. He taught us to behave well, lead good lives and avoid evil things. He would repeat to us the proverb: 'Only Heaven can bring you great riches, but moderate riches can be won by hard work.' And although we were poor our parents would always manage to get us new clothes for New Year and the house would be decorated.

How did we manage when the harvest was bad? We would set out before sunrise and walk to the mountains to cut grass; then we would carry the bundles to the market town to sell them. The grass would be dried and burned and the ash used in making pottery. Sometimes we would go into the forests to cut firewood. It was cold and dark under the trees but we would have to keep chopping until we had enough wood to sell. It was hard work for little return. But one good thing I remember was the way local people would bring hot tea and rice cakes at midday to sell quite cheaply. That helped us keep going.

When I was twenty-four I was married in the traditional way, without ever seeing my husband before the wedding. Yes, I was scared, wondering what my fate would be, although my parents had made inquiries. My husband belonged to a wealthy family — why, his great grandfather had even been kidnapped, he was so rich! But my marriage was not happy. My parents-in-law did not treat me well. My husband smoked opium and never gave me a cent of pocket-money. I was sent out to work. I bore him a son but I was not allowed to look after him properly. Instead they sent me into the mountains to cut grass; and not long before the baby's first hundred days, he was allowed to die of neglect while I was away, working.

In my grief and fury, I ran away. I came to Hong Kong and found work sorting Chinese medicine for twenty dollars a month — and three of that went on a bed-space in Taihang village. My parents-in-law sent some ruffians after me. They told me I'd be in for a lot of trouble if I didn't return to my husband. But I told them to get lost! As for my husband, I said 'Tell him to give up opium and try to behave himself'. I would have nothing more to do with him. Well, I had no more trouble from them, but soon afterwards I lost my sorting job and got work as a coolie out at Shamshuipo handling boxes of foodstuff at the army barracks. It was heavy work, but I was strong enough. I made good friends among the women and they suggested I seek work as an amah.

Soon I was fixed up for three months with a British army family as a learner-amah under the 'Number One' houseboy. I learned washing and ironing and other amah chores — even some

*Cheung Te*

cooking. Then after three months the 'Number One' told me there was nothing more for me and I would have to go. The master had given him money for my wages, but he cheated and kept it all for himself. But I had learned the job and from then on I worked for army families and they treated me very nicely.

I can't bear to even think about the Cultural Revolution and the Red Guards. I only learned later what they did to my parents back home. The gangs came into our house and treated them — I just can't describe it. They tortured them and then they killed them. Yes, my parents were poor peasants, not so-called capitalist roaders. But we had this bit of land, and somebody laid false information against them. It is too terrible, I can't speak about it.

My younger brother survived. He was studying in Shumchun at the time and he got his principal to give him a certificate of good conduct. And it seems this saved him. He is all that is left to me. I cling to him and his wife and their three daughters. Things are not easy in China and I send him money to help. I tell him to be a good and responsible father, to look after his children, and be content with what he has. He needn't worry about money. I will always try to help.

As for me, I went on working as an amah. For years I worked for a German gentleman and his wife. When he was transferred by his firm to Britain, they took me with them. Yes, imagine it — I travelled in an aeroplane, sitting in a First Class window seat with plenty of room to stretch, looking out on the whole world! But I didn't stay in England very long. I couldn't stand the cold weather. After nine months I had to ask to be allowed to return here, where I managed to find another job as an amah.

By then my sight was beginning to fail. I went to a doctor but he could do no good. Then my brother asked me to go to Kwangtung because near his home was a very good eye-doctor. So I went and had treatment — I had to take some special herbs. And I'm glad to say this cured me. My eyes brightened up again and now I can see quite well. Unfortunately the doctor was very old and he passed away soon afterwards. Even the prescription he gave me is lost. It was destroyed along with my other things in a bad typhoon.

When I was too old to work I paid a thousand dollars for a hut on the roof of a building in Canton Road and lived there for some years. Later the government developed that area and the Social Welfare Department arranged for me to come and live here. I keep in close touch with my young brother. He is all I have. He came here from China to see me only yesterday.

# *Mother's favourite*

**M**y family were farming people. They were Hakkas with plenty of money and land. I had seven brothers and one sister. I was the youngest and my mother liked me the best. Whenever there was extra money from raising pigs or growing vegetables she kept it for me. She spoiled me, but how was I to know? My early life was one of ease and comfort. I went to school and studied the Four Books. But I never studied hard. Now, at seventy-five I can hardly read a newspaper.

Do you know about Hakka people and their customs? In our village, if you had money, you were married by arrangement at the age of eight. A wife was bought, usually from a neighbouring village, and there was a wedding feast. My marriage was never consummated. My wife grew up with me from when we were eight and mostly we played together. I have no idea what became of her later.

My father died a few years before the Japanese occupation. All his sons were married by that time and the land, as is customary in Hakka villages, was shared out between us. But because my mother had money, she bought extra land for me, so I had more than the others.

My brothers didn't care too much. We were, all of us, an idle lot. Some of my brothers spent their days smoking opium — we grew the poppies ourselves. Most of them gambled and some gambled all their land away. Only one or two of my brothers farmed themselves. As for me, I never worked with my hands and only supervised the labour of others. My mother would not allow me to work. So later, when I needed to, I didn't know how. My mother loved me too much.

Times turned bad when the Japanese came to our village in Waiyeung County. Because I was rich and had plenty of land they arrested me. First they demanded food, eggs in particular, and that wasn't easy. Then they wanted me to procure women. They gave me money and insisted that I find virgins for them. They threatened to cut my head off if I didn't co-operate. I don't want to talk about this. I had a horrible time!

When the People's Liberation Army arrived, I was in even worse trouble. I was strung up for a whole day with my arms tied above me. People spat and yelled at me. But when darkness fell, one of my brothers came secretly and cut me down. I ran away that very night. Much later, my sister wrote to say that my mother had hanged herself. She was eighty then.

I have been in Hong Kong for almost forty years now and all the time I have been on my own. With no working experience and little education I had to take the lowest jobs. You name it and I've probably done it! I collected newspapers, I gathered tins, I scavenged in dustbins. Anything just to earn a meal.

For a while I pushed coal carts and earned two or three dollars a day; but it wasn't enough to eat on. I worked as a caretaker in a building, but again I only received three dollars a day and nearly starved. I tried to become a coolie; but if you don't know how to carry a load with a pole, you drop things and people won't hire you. I learned to weed from farmers in the New Territories. I worked on construction sites. I have even been a night-soil collector.

*Leung Lai*

During most of this time I had no hope. When I had the money, I would rent a bed for a night; when I had none I would sleep on the streets. Sometimes the police would move me on. Sometimes I would find a spot where nobody bothered me. My best time was when I found work in a tea-house a few years ago. I earned more than a thousand a month, was fed and given a place to sleep. Then I had a stroke and they said I was too old to continue.

I have not heard from my family in China for many years. Once I sent a bit of money home, but my sister wrote and said never to send anything again. Her oldest son had been arrested for questioning and she said that once again I had brought trouble upon the family. So now I know nothing about my old home, not even whether anyone there is still alive.

On lonely evenings I remember my mother.

# *Suicides every day*

**M**y family is from Toishan in Kwangtung Province. But I was born in Hong Kong in 1926. My birth was recorded so I had no trouble getting back into Hong Kong over fifty years later. When I was young we travelled all over China. My father died when I was five and my mother took me and my three-year-old sister to live with my uncle, her younger brother, who worked for the railways in Hankow. We were a middle-class family and for those days quite well-off. Our mother, who had received an excellent education, was determined that we should have the same. My sister and I were sent to a Catholic school where we studied both English and Chinese.

Towards the end of my primary school education my uncle was transferred to Tsingtao. Again we followed him and continued our studies at the local school. Then came the Japanese war and we began to move about a great deal, always running away from the soldiers. There was much confusion. The Japanese seemed to turn up just everywhere and nobody ever quite knew where to go next. To make things worse, there was widespread famine in the countryside. I saw people begging for food and sometimes dying along the roadside. Even today those memories trouble me.

In 1946, after the Japanese had surrendered, my uncle was transferred to Shanghai and my mother and I followed him. My sister went overseas to study — first to India, where we had strong family connections, and then to Hong Kong. In 1954 she emigrated to the United States. My mother and I remained in China. I finished secondary school and then trained to become a nurse. Later, having qualified as a midwife as well, I got myself a job in a big urban hospital in Shanghai. I enjoyed my work and my mother was content.

During the years of the Great Leap Forward our lives became very difficult. There was no food and my mother ended up eating horsemeat and other such unspeakable things. I was given meals in hospital. The food was poor — but at least I ate. My mother was in a bad way though; she grew thinner day by day. Her face was pale and her hands began to tremble. I was very distressed to see her getting worse without being able to help.

In 1962 I applied for my mother to move to Hong Kong. At that time it was relatively easy for elderly people to obtain an exit visa from China. Our government regarded them as 'useless eaters' and was glad to be rid of them. My mother had no problem in obtaining the necessary papers. For me, as a professional, it would have been more difficult to leave, even though I was born in Hong Kong. But Shanghai had become my home and I was happy there.

My world changed totally with the Cultural Revolution that began in 1966. Life became chaotic — dangerous if you didn't know your way around. But it was difficult to know where to turn. The staff at our hospital had split into two factions: one proclaiming loyalty to the Party and the city administration, the other supporting the so-called Revolutionary Headquarters. Both factions claimed to support Chairman Mao, and we all competed to be first and best in 'eliminating old customs, ideas and cultures' or in 'wiping out all ghosts and monsters'. But who was to know who were the 'ghosts and monsters'? We spent a great deal of our time on the streets reading big-character

*Virginia Lieu*

posters and keeping up with developments and with the latest slogans, which we would then shout at each other. We would write our own posters and attack one another. The administrators were particularly badly treated and some, even doctors, were forced to do lowly jobs like washing floors and cleaning lavatories.

For well over a year the hospital was more or less closed. Although we continued to receive our salaries we stopped nursing altogether. Ordinary cases were refused admission and emergencies were handled only by some nurses who simply couldn't bear to see the really sick uncared for. But still the patients kept coming. There were many people who were badly beaten up and — every day — there were suicides. All over Shanghai people were killing themselves. Some of them had been long-time party members, but had come under attack for their class background. Others had been denounced for their past or present political associations. At our hospital there were several nurses who had supported the Kuomintang before the Communists took over. They also committed suicide. I was very frightened for myself. As you know, I have a bourgeois class background and could easily have attracted attention. But I kept my head down and shouted with the others. I was lucky, nobody took any notice of me.

In 1971, when things had calmed down a bit, I received word that my mother was ill in Hong Kong. I applied for permission to join her but this was refused. I said to the officials: 'I am a native of Hong Kong. My mother is ill and I am obliged to look after her. So why not let me go?' But they said no. They gave me no reason; they just turned me down. Finally, in 1976, I was allowed to apply. It took the Chinese authorities a full two years to process my papers. But the Hong Kong Government let me enter without any fuss. I came to Hong Kong in 1978. I was allowed to bring out my savings, over two thousand Renminbi. But my mother had died meanwhile.

I have lived in Hong Kong for almost ten years now but came to this hostel only recently. I have a room of my own but although I am quite comfortable I don't intend to stay. My sister in America will be retiring soon and wants to come to Hong Kong. She plans to rent a small apartment and we shall live together. That will be much better than being alone.

# *Why go home?*

犸
仕
根

**I** was born in 1904 during the reign of Emperor Kuang Hsu. My father was a farmer who worked his own land in Shuntak. He was a gambler though; all he ever cared about was *fan-tan*. In slack farming seasons he would gamble day and night. He would lose whatever money he earned. When debt collectors came, he took to his bed and paid no attention. He would pretend he was ill. My mother died early. My father never bothered about me and I was raised by an aunt. I went to school for five years. I can still read and write a little. Not much to boast about though, is it?

When I was eighteen my godmother's daughter took me to Singapore where I found work as a deckhand on a ship going to Hong Kong and China. In between jobs I would work as a coolie. I got married in China at the age of twenty-two. I was so poor — I barely managed to invite two tables of friends. We cooked the wedding dinner ourselves.

Then my sister married a seaman, a 'Number One' for Taikoo Swire in Canton. He introduced me to the company and I was given work as a cook on a boat going from Swatow to Hong Kong. I made money smuggling. We bought sugar in Hong Kong and sold it in Swatow. For me there was no big profit, but it helped make a living.

I was in Shanghai in 1937 when the Japanese soldiers came. The harbour was crowded with refugees. People were struggling with each other, pushing and falling into the sea. Everybody wanted to come aboard because we were sailing for Hong Kong. We were jammed to the top. I gave my bunk space to a woman. I thought of my wife and felt sorry for her. Somebody else offered me money for that space but I said it was not for sale. I could have taken thirty yuan for it and that was a month's pay. Perhaps I was stupid.

During the Japanese war I continued to work as a seaman. We went to Cape Town, Vancouver and many other ports. It is curious to think that I saw the world during the war. Once I had a lucky escape. We were on our way to Colombo and three planes strafed us. They kept on coming back and we were quite badly hit. Some sailors were hurt, some killed. We didn't sink; but I decided that I had trusted my luck for long enough. I left the sea and went back to my village where I worked on the land.

I came to Hong Kong in 1958. At that time all peasants in China had to join communes and we all had to eat in communal dining halls. I didn't see the point and the food was very poor. That's why I left. For more than ten years I worked in a *dim-sum* restaurant. Then, through a friend, I got a job as a dishwasher at a well-known restaurant in Nathan Road in Kowloon. I was paid one hundred and fifty dollars a month and was there for a year.

Yes, I tried my hand at many things. In the Seventies, I farmed for several years in the New Territories. One year we were flooded and all our vegetables were destroyed. I didn't make a single dollar that season.

There have always been ups and downs in my life. If I had money I would send some back to my wife. If I lost my job I would return to China for a while. My wife was farming and also worked

*Fung See-kan*

in the communal kitchens. I'd stay for a bit and then come back to Hong Kong where I'd bum off some of my friends while looking for work again.

I have only one son. He finished middle school and now is a steel worker in China. He has two children and my wife helps to look after them. My daughter-in-law is alright but very fierce. You know, times have changed. It used to be that a daughter was given to her husband's family and she would be obedient to her in-laws. Nowadays, a son serves his mother-in-law rather than the mother who raised him. I had to pay seven thousand dollars for my son's wedding!

I still go home to China for New Year occasionally. Food is plentiful at that time. Fish is cheap, there is a lot of it, and you don't need to buy vegetables because everyone has private plots.

My wife wants me to return for good. If I died in Hong Kong nobody would know and nobody would mourn me, she says. I say 'Why go home in my old age? All they'd give me if I went to China is two meals a day!' Here, in Hong Kong, the government lets me have money for my own use. I have a room and plenty to eat. At New Year, if I stay, I get several hundred dollars of *laisee* money at this place. I don't intend to return to China at the moment. But I will see how things go.

# *So long ago*

I was born in a village near Canton City. I hardly knew my father. He spent most of his time overseas in Cuba. He had gone there with his own father and helped him run a jewellery business. My mother didn't seem to mind his long absences and we always had enough to eat. My father sent money home and we had servants who cooked and cleaned the house. On one of his trips back, my father brought me a necklace of pearls — he said Cuba was famous for them. It was the only thing I recall him ever giving me. But I didn't have it for long as it was stolen.

My mother bore him five children, but she was not his only wife. One year he came back with my grandfather and brought several exotic-looking ladies. They were introduced as my father's other wives. I was curious and wanted to ask him many questions, but my mother told me to be quiet or my father would beat me. During this visit my grandfather held a big celebration. It would not do to have just the servants cooking. We rented a banquet hall in a famous restaurant. There was as much food as at a wedding reception. It is one of the few good memories from my childhood.

When I was six or seven years old my mother's sister had me brought from Canton to live with her in Hong Kong. She had never married and she looked on me as her daughter, and even planned to leave me all she had when she died. My aunt worked as an amah for a foreign family in Hong Kong. Sometimes she would bring home scraps of food from their table. I never met them. We lived in a small flat on Robinson Road and she would go back and forth every day to her employers. I spent my days cooking or mending and put aside any thought of going to school. It would have been a luxury for me.

Then the Japanese invaded northern China in 1937 and my aunt decided we should return as quickly as possible to my family in Canton. We went on foot by way of Kowloon and Shumchun. Many others were going the same way. We had no food and eventually my aunt could go no further. I had to leave her by the roadside and go on alone, clutching a picture of my family and asking for directions along the way. I travelled for many days and nights, and my arrival home coincided with another cause for celebration — my father had returned again from Cuba.

But then the Japanese attacked Canton. During the fighting before the city was captured, my mother and father and my baby brother and I were hiding in a neighbour's cellar. My brother must have sensed danger for he began to cry. My father said he would go and get him something to eat. But as my father climbed out of the cellar he was shot twice in the back by the Japanese and killed. When we came out of hiding the Japanese wouldn't let us bury the dead. For days we had to walk past our father's corpse — and many others which were strewn on the roads. But I was only fifteen at the time and my father's death just seemed to me like anyone else's.

About a year later it was decided that I should be married. The family put my mother's elder sister in charge of finding a suitable husband. I knew little about the man they chose, except that he came from a well-to-do family who also had interests in Cuba. He was the only son in his family, a butcher who lived in a village about half-way between Canton and Hong Kong. I spent

*Kwan Loi*

the first few months of my marriage sleeping with my mother-in-law, because I had not yet begun to bleed. Then my husband came to me and soon I was pregnant.

The baby was due at about the time Hong Kong was bombed by the Japanese, at the end of 1941. Bombs and shells were falling close to us and it was hard to make a living, even for a family as well-to-do as ours. We had little food and I remember being so frightened by explosions that I was always running into the banana groves and canefields when there was a bang. Late one evening the bombs frightened me so much that I ran out into a field and there gave birth to my baby, on my own. I think I must have become a little mad after that because I remember losing track of where I was. I was cold and hungry and had no food. I was so under-nourished that I had little milk for my baby, a little boy, and he died after six days. I almost died from exposure myself and remember swimming across a pond and lying full length on the back of a cow for warmth.

Later I gave birth to another boy who lived until he was five. Shortly after he was born my husband decided we should leave Canton, where we were then living. The war had so ravaged the city that many people were leaving. My husband had little work and decided that we should join some distant relatives in Mui Wo on Lantau Island. My mother-in-law had already died of malnutrition and we had no alternative but to leave.

When we arrived in Mui Wo my husband had to give up being a butcher and he became a market gardener. We joined up with some other families to fix up an old house which we all lived in. The Japanese were still around. I heard many stories about the soldiers raping women. If they resisted, the Japanese cut the lower part of their body in two. We did not stay long in Mui Wo because it was too crowded. We moved to nearby Peng Chau and stayed there for almost thirty years. We had seven children. All but three of them are dead now. I have one daughter who often takes me out regularly for *dim-sum*.

You asked whether I keep in touch with other relatives. I'm afraid that at sixty-five my memory is bad and I'm not sure what happened to them. I never really knew my younger brothers and sisters, and most of the photographs of them have been lost. I heard that one of my brothers is a policeman in Peking, but I've never met him and only know that he has six daughters and three sons. My mother is still alive in China. She will be eighty-five soon. My life in China all seems such a long time ago.

# *Medicine man*

符榮基

**I** was born in the Ching dynasty — during the reign of the Emperor Kuang Hsu, which ended in 1908. I don't remember much about the Revolution, except that my father took me to the barber's shop where we both had our queues cut off. Otherwise, people would just stop you in the street and snip off your hair. Those who had no money cut their own hair at home.

My father was a peasant who owned his own land in Sunhing County and we were not too badly off. He sent me to school for a few years, so I can read a little. When I was eighteen a marriage was arranged through a matchmaker in our village. Then I came to Hong Kong. There was no real border in those days. I just took a train. Of course, Hong Kong looked different then. I remember the tram road, Des Voeux Road, being on the waterfront. Later they filled in the sea to reclaim the land.

Did I tell you that I worked for a Chinese medicine shop in the village? When I came to Hong Kong, friends from the village helped me find the same kind of work here. It was easy to learn in those days. In the beginning, like everyone else, I did minor chores. I cleaned up, made tea and did odd jobs. I watched experienced workers and learned the names of the many plants and animals which are commonly used in Chinese medicine. Later I was allowed to make up prescriptions, which called for all sorts of ingredients — bark, dried chrysanthemums, cockroaches and even seahorses. These mixtures would have to be boiled and the extract often tastes bitter. We used to pack dried plums and raisins with the medicine to 'sweeten the tongue' after it had been taken.

I got paid three dollars a month when I first started work, but I was also given room and board. Over the years I worked in many medicine shops, moving on when the pay was better elsewhere. I worked for more than sixty years and when I stopped, at the age of seventy-eight, I was earning two thousand two hundred a month plus food and a room of my own. My wife never liked it in Hong Kong. She remained in our village where she could farm. I would visit her every year. We had one daughter, who is now dead, and there are grandchildren who sometimes write.

I was in Hong Kong at the start of the war, but when the Japanese came I went back to the village to look after my farm. Luckily, we didn't have much trouble and there was enough to eat.

The main danger was of being caught by the Japanese soldiers and forced to work as a coolie. But not me! There was always some warning. We would see them coming and would run and hide in the woods or on the hillside. Sometimes the soldiers would be angry; they would hammer on the walls of our houses and break down the doors. They would take the chickens, pigs or anything they could find. When they caught someone they would take him away. Some men managed to escape and come back to the village. Some never returned.

After the war ended, I came back to Hong Kong and I worked and lived in a herbal medicine shop in Wanchai. When I retired, I rented a bed-space with a dozen or so other people sharing a room. I lived there for five or six years until the landlord repossessed the flat. Now I live in this home.

You know, the days don't change much. I'm now eighty-nine but I can still help a bit with

*Fu Wing-kay*

people's coughs, colds, aches and pains by advising what herbal medicine they ought to take. Every morning I walk and exercise a bit. Every evening I watch TV. My grandson invited me back to our village last year when he was married, but there is no one there I know any more. Most of my friends are dead. At Ching Ming festival I go across the border to visit our family's ancestral graves. At holidays I buy a bit more food. Otherwise, one day is the same as another.

# Too handsome a husband

**S**it down Miss, so I can have a good look at you. It's rare for us old folks to have a chance to talk to a pretty lady such as you. And tell that young man of yours to make sure those photos he's taking of me come out real good. I know I'm an old hag now. But in my day, when I was young — younger even than you are now — I was by far the prettiest girl around. You may well think that I'm boasting now. But what I'm telling you is true.

You see, on the first and fifteenth day of each moon it was customary for us village girls to light joss-sticks in the temple. We would dress our hair and wear our embroidered *kwa* for those visits. And on each occasion all the men of the village would line up along the sides of the temple and watch us. They were quite shameless. They would call out who were the most beautiful girls and who were the plain and the ugly ones. I'd hide my face behind my fan and keep my eyes down. But I became well known for my beauty and people said any man would be lucky to marry such a pretty girl.

My name is Mak See. I'm eighty-six years old now and I come from Taiping in Tungkwun County. My father was a wealthy farmer. He had two oxen to work the fields and he also raised pigs — enough to leave two or three a year for ourselves. We also kept chickens and ducks and had fresh eggs to eat. My father had four wives in all. The first wife, my mother, bore him three daughters, and I was the youngest of them. Poor mother! She was given no pork when she gave birth to us girls as she was expected to produce a son. This punishment had been laid down by the village headman. But number two wife and number three wife were treated even worse. They had no children at all. My father and his mother scolded them all the time. So finally they ran away. Then my father took yet another wife. This number four wife gave him a son.

My family owned two houses. In those days the size of a house was measured by the number of bricks across the living-room which ran along the front. Normally houses were nine bricks wide. My father's houses were eleven and fifteen bricks wide. My mother and we three daughters stayed in the first house; the other wives and later the son lived in the second house. None of my mothers had bound feet. I expect it was because they had to work in the fields. I never did, because I was considered too young for such work and I just helped at home. But I never went to school either, because there were no teachers in the village.

I was married when I was twenty. I didn't really want to be married, but my older sister forced me to. One day this matchmaker came to my father and said she had found the right husband for me. And that's how it was done. I first learned my future husband's name and age when our birthdates were matched for harmony. He was said to be good-looking and my sisters teased me about this. But what's so special about marrying a handsome man? After all, wasn't I a very pretty girl? So I kept my head high and smiled for the world to see. But inwardly I grew more and more fearful as my wedding day approached. I was going to leave my home and my village to live with a complete stranger. What would he be like and how would I be treated by his family?

Wedding presents were exchanged. There was a lot of food — roasted pigs, cakes, sweets and other such things. I received a jade bracelet with gold trimmings and a gold wedding ring. Look — I still wear the bracelet. But the ring is gone. I had it melted down during the war to buy food. I wore a new *kwa* on my wedding day. My sisters had given it to me and it was embroidered in red and green. I wore red cloth shoes, white socks and carried a white fan. My head-dress was of black satin and was beautifully embroidered in many colours. It was held in place by golden hairpins.

When the right hour had come my husband's family sent a red sedan-chair from their village to carry me to his home. There were firecrackers and even a band playing. It was truly a festive occasion. My husband's family house was big. In fact it was larger than my father's houses — sixteen bricks across the living-room. I arrived at this house in my sedan-chair and was carried straight into the bedroom. There I just sat and everybody came in to have a look at me.

The first time I saw my husband was on my wedding night. I was very frightened and really scared of him. It was so awful to be sitting right next to a man. I hardly dared raise my eyes to him. Finally I looked up. He smiled at me. He was about ten years older than me and really very handsome. You know, he almost looked European. No, he was not of mixed blood. He was just very good-looking, very tall and he was also very kind to me. After a few days I overcame my shyness and was not afraid of him any more.

I don't know if my husband had known other women before our marriage; it was no concern of mine. But as for us, we never even held hands. We slept separately. I mean he had his own comforter, or quilt, and I had mine. During all my married life I never even once shared a comforter with my husband. Of course, we never had any children. I told the matchmaker that it had been a mistake to find me such a handsome husband. She lived next door and I scolded her often.

My husband and a few other people ran a chain of gambling dens. Many people gambled there every evening until midnight. But I never went. Women weren't normally allowed there — and in any case my husband said that if he allowed me to play a few numbers and I should win, people would accuse him of having given me inside information. But at home I was totally in charge. Only my father-in-law lived with us and my husband let me run the household as I saw fit. He bought whatever we liked to eat from the market — rice, vegetables, oil and meat. There was always plenty of food. I never had to sew clothes for him either. He bought ready-to-wear things, including western suits. Yes, he was a very modern man, so he was. We had been married for about four years when my husband suddenly died. He had run up a lot of debts in the gambling dens and I was told that he had left me no money. All at once, I was very poor.

For a few months I supported myself by working in the fields. But I was not used to that kind of work and hated it. Finally I decided to come to Hong Kong to make a living. I left my village at eight in the morning, took a boat and arrived in Hong Kong around six the same evening. Somehow I found work on a construction site, mixing cement and concrete. It was hard and dirty work. Then a relative introduced me to a job in a restaurant. I washed vegetables and slaughtered

*Mak See*

chickens and ducks. I knew how to do all this from my life in the village. So I was quite content. In fact I have been employed in restaurant kitchens for most of my working life.

Now, of course, I am old and my fingers are too stiff and crooked to do that sort of work. I haven't been in this home for very long though. I was living in a little cubicle, all on my own, in a housing estate when this priest came and said that he could help me. He introduced me to the manager of Helping Hand and that's how I finally came here. I'll tell you though, Miss, that I'm very comfortable here. Of all the places I have been to this is the best. I'm sorry you have to leave now. Please come and see me again, when you have the time. Take care, take care!

# *Wasting good iron on a nail*

**T**hank you for asking me to talk to you. I am afraid of wasting your time. I am old, uneducated and have no culture. There's little I can tell you.

My name is Yuen Pui. I was born in Hoifung seventy-two years ago. My father was a fisherman. Besides my parents there was my father's mother and my elder sister. Five of us lived in a hut.

When I was four my mother died; when I was nine my grandmother died; when I was eleven my father died. My elder sister was nineteen then. She made her living by catching crabs and molluscs in the sand. I helped as best I could until, at the age of thirteen, I became a cowherd. We managed to eat but life was hard.

I was about seventeen when the war with Japan began and I decided to enlist. As you will know, in China soldiers have always been held in low regard. People say 'You don't waste good iron on a nail and you don't waste a good man as a soldier!' But then, who was I? Joining the army meant I would be fed and clothed. They even paid me a small wage!

I was sent to Tsingtao in Shantung for training. There were about two hundred recruits in my company and I didn't have too bad a time. One of my comrades even taught me how to play the fiddle and I have enjoyed music ever since. But after a year, and before I had ever seen a Japanese soldier, I deserted. You will think 'What a wastrel', and I guess you are right. But you see, I suddenly realised that since I was the only son it would be the end of our line if I were to be killed. There would be no one left to pay respect to our ancestors; surely, that could not be right. So I returned to our village in Kwangtung Province. There was no problem. No one ever bothered to look for me and I went back to doing odd jobs.

Now I will tell you about the worst thing I can remember in my life. It happened in 1947. There was a terrible typhoon. The sea came right over our paddy fields and there was no harvest. We didn't even have enough food for one meal every other day. There were two thousand people in the village, two-thirds of whom died either in that storm or of starvation. They were just buried in the ground — no one had money for a coffin. Lots of parents gave their sons away and their daughters were married off to other villages. My sister and I collected salt in exchange for a little food. We had to wait a whole year for the next harvest.

The best time I have ever had was when I got married a few years after the typhoon. It was not an arranged marriage. My wife was a farmer's daughter. We had met working and had grown to like each other. So after a while we simply moved in together. We had a son and for some years life passed well enough. But then my wife began to complain. I didn't earn much and at times there wasn't enough to eat. She kept nagging me. Finally, in 1953, she got fed up and walked out on me. She left our three-year-old son behind. I have not seen or heard from her since. I guess I can't blame her really; I hadn't supported her well; I hadn't been much of a husband.

In 1956 I decided to come to Hong Kong because I couldn't find any work in the village. I left my son with my sister. But it was no longer easy to enter Hong Kong. So I came here as an illegal immigrant. I sneaked into Hong Kong in a twelve-foot boat, rowing all the way. It was quite a

*Yuen Pui*

dangerous journey. The sea was rough and the stern of the boat would shoot up high out of the water and the bow went deep down. There were five of us, all men, and it took us two days to reach Hong Kong. But do you know, we climbed ashore at Jordan Road without any trouble of any sort. We never met a policeman or any other official. Guess I was lucky for once!

Life in Hong Kong was better than in the village. For a few years I found employment as a tea-house boy. I didn't earn much in that job -- about a hundred dollars a month -- but I was fed. Mostly I worked as a coolie though. Now and then I would send a little money back for my son.

No, I never married again. Who'd have wanted a good-for-nothing coolie anyhow? And now I can't even do that sort of work any more. I have lost my strength and live in an old people's home. Sometimes I dream, however. I dream that I could be a watchman in a big factory or warehouse. Would I fall asleep on the job? Well, old people do snooze and doze off. But then, if I could find such a job, I would probably be kept awake by the responsibility. Well, anyhow, it's just a dream ....

I really am quite a loner. My son has remained in China and I have not seen him for many years. He is a duck-farmer now. He used to write to me but I never let him have my new address when I moved here. Now I haven't heard from him for over a year. I have no money to send him anyhow.

I don't intend to return to my village; I would only be a nuisance to my family. It was my sister who really brought up my son. He wasn't married a few years ago and I don't know whether he is now. It would be nice to know I had a grandson. Otherwise I don't have any hopes or expectations. Death may come anytime.

# *Convent girl*

**M**y aunt carried me to the nuns at a convent in Kowloon when I was five, in 1917. The sores in my eyes were blinding me. I was so sick I almost died. I have no other relatives I know of. The nuns said that my aunt, who was my father's sister, worked for a priest who spread the gospel. She was a Catholic — that was why she took me to the convent. Then she went away with the priest and never came back.

I wish I could remember my past. I wish I knew where I came from. There were so many sick children in the convent then. Perhaps my mother came and asked for me and the nuns said I had died. Perhaps I was not wanted. How does anyone know? I was baptised and I stayed with the nuns for over twenty years. No, I can't read or write. The nuns said there was no need for girls to study, even though we wanted to. They said 'Why study, when you have to go to work anyhow?' But they taught us how to sew and we made church vestments and altar cloths. They were good to us.

When I was a teenager, fifteen or sixteen maybe, I followed the nuns to Canada. There were five of us who lived together as a family. We stayed in a convent in Montreal and spent our days sewing. We were given food and lodging and earned several dollars a week. I was happy then. Even today I know a little French. After four or five years I had to come back to Hong Kong by myself. My eyes had been injured in an accident and, despite an operation, they didn't improve. In the end the doctor advised me to return to Hong Kong as the cold in Canada might damage my eyes permanently. It was sad to be parted from my friends.

I left the convent when I was in my late twenties. The nuns had given me good references and I easily found work here as an amah looking after children. The family I remember best was English. I took care of a little red-haired girl. Her name was Lily. She was five years old when I first joined them and very sweet. I often wonder what became of her.

After the Japanese came to Hong Kong I fled with some friends into the countryside in China, where I stayed for four years. It was not too bad to start with. We grew vegetables, raised chickens and pigs, and collected grass and firewood in the mountains. During the last year of our stay the Japanese came to our village. There were about seven or eight of us when they stopped us for the first time. They asked where our husbands were. I was very frightened. I said that my husband had died in Canton. I didn't know what else to say, so I just said he was dead. They asked my friends, all Hakkas, the same question. They were looking for men. They came every day. They took our vegetables, pigs, chickens, even peanuts — everything. We had no food left. We dug up roots to eat. We were lucky that the Japanese soldiers came to our village so late in the war.

When peace came I returned to Hong Kong. As I had learned no other skills I worked as an amah and, later, while I was still strong enough, as a cleaning woman. My last job was in a school. I worked there for six years, cleaning, washing the blackboards, scrubbing the floors. Even though I was not supposed to, I lived there. In the evenings I would push the desks together and sleep on them as if on a bed. I pushed them back in the mornings. I stopped working in the school when

*Anna Wong*

the owner closed it.

I had only been paid a little over a hundred dollars a month, so I had few savings. I lived on what I had and stayed with friends — a few nights here, a few nights there. Finally my money was finished and I had to ask for Welfare. In the beginning I was given two hundred and twenty dollars a month. Now it is more. I have been on Public Assistance for six or seven years. Before I came to this place, I rented a room for a hundred dollars a month but the rent went up to two hundred and thirty dollars, which I couldn't afford.

Somebody told me about this home so I came to see it and applied for admission. The people here are very pleasant. We help one another — I like it. I still go to church often. I watch television a little and cook my own meals. I enjoy sewing and knitting, but my eyes are very weak. The doctor tells me that I have cataracts, but that it is too early to have an operation. He has not told me yet when I may have it. Medical treatment is very troublesome. It takes a day's queuing before the doctor can see you. Luckily I have time.

# *Dairy Farm days*

I was born in 1915 in the staff quarters of the Dairy Farm at Pokfulam. It was a simple home; but you have to remember that if you were a working man in Hong Kong in those days and needed a place to live, you had to find wood and other materials and build it yourself. So being in staff quarters was a big advantage. As a boy I was sent to the nearest village school and learned some basic Chinese; but I only stayed two years. I didn't get on at school. I simply quit.

My father retired from the Dairy Farm in 1932. By that time he was earning forty-five dollars a month, and we considered ourselves a middle-class family. I had joined the farm as an assistant cowman, doing the dirty work; but when my father retired, I was lucky enough to be given his job as a foreman. I felt a fool for not having learned more at school, and I taught myself the characters in my spare time. I married at twenty-two. The girl was a neighbour working at the Dairy Farm and so it happened fairly naturally. We had two children and were happy enough.

Then the war came and the Japanese. One of the things the Japanese did was to move the Dairy Farm down to Hainan Island, far to the south of here. Why did they do such a thing? Well, they had military and naval bases down there and they wanted the milk and meat for the troops.

It was not a very sensible idea. The Hainan climate is tropical and there isn't good pasture; so much of the herd was lost. But what was far worse for me was that my wife died giving birth to our third son. So I was left with three small boys to look after, including the baby.

How did the war end for me? Well, one day in 1945 the Japanese came to us and said they had lost the war and had surrendered to China; they said that we should stay behind and that all property would be handled by the Chinese authorities. So we came under Chinese military control; pay became very irregular; and life in general was very rough. After six months of chaos, United Nations officials concerned with refugees arrived, interviewed us and arranged for free passages back to Hong Kong. I left the baby behind in Hainan with some people there.

Back in Hong Kong, things were rough as well. Luckily, a friend of mine had a job working in the garden of a millionaire. He had a hut in the garden where I was able to stay with my sons. I would leave them there during the day while I worked down in Aberdeen, painting boats and returning with food in the evening.

Then I learned to drive and got a licence; the test was very simple then. I started driving a taxi and later got a job with a textile company which had a mill out at Tuenmun. By then I was able to rent a place at Causeway Bay and send my sons to boarding school. But I could never earn enough to send them to middle school: that is my great regret. The cotton mill went broke, so that was the end of that job. Then I worked for a while as a relief lorry-driver earning four hundred and fifty dollars a month.

The big event in the late Fifties was the recruitment of Hong Kong workers, including drivers, to return to mainland China on three-year contracts to work for 'National Reconstruction'. I believe as many as a hundred thousand Hong Kong workers responded to that call, including about twenty

*Cho Sang*

thousand drivers. I went to China in 1958 and returned in 1961. The first two years there were pretty good. Many of the Hong Kong workers were sent to faraway places; but I stayed at a technical training centre in Kwangtung Province teaching new drivers and I was treated well.

But by the third year, the food situation there had become desperate. I was asked whether I would renew my contract and continue to serve my country. They were very polite to me; but I felt it was impossible under those conditions, and I returned to Hong Kong. Not that things were that easy here. I drove a *pak pai*, an illegal taxi, renting it from the owner and making no more than twenty dollars a day. Later I worked as a relief driver on a fourteen-seater light bus.

When I got old and couldn't earn enough to live on, I was fully supported by my sons, who were both working in restaurants. They paid the monthly rent for a small flat in Tsuenwan; but every year the landlord increased the rent until it was simply too much. I talked to the Kai Fong Citizens Association about it; they put me in touch with the Social Welfare Department, and that's how I've come here.

I never married again after my wife died. I have come to think of myself as a single man by nature. You may say mine has not been an easy life, but I don't complain. I have two sons and three grandchildren — two of them male.

# *An empty promise*

陈
伍

**I**f you want to know my real name, it's Chan Ng. And I'm eighty-seven years old. My father called me Ng because it means five and I was the fifth child born to our family. But it was not a pretty name and it didn't have any propitious meaning. So when I grew up I consulted a fortune teller to help me find a name that would be both attractive and auspicious for my future life. The astrologer studied my birthdate carefully. He asked me many questions and examined my facial features. Finally he told me that as I was born with fire, I should adopt a name connected with water, so that I would lead an easy and harmonious life. So I chose the name Wai-ping, which means Magnificent Lotus, the lily that floats on the water.

But the fortune teller's predictions proved to be wrong, or perhaps some jealous spirits interfered and kept me from enjoying the prosperous and peaceful life I had been meant to enjoy. When I was young things were not too bad. My father had a store in Hong Kong, selling oil, rice and other basic supplies. It was a family business, run with no outside help. There was enough income to support our family quite comfortably, and I was even sent to school from the age of seven to thirteen. But then my father became seriously ill and decided to return to his native village. I went with him and helped to look after him until he died.

A few months later I returned to Hong Kong. I wanted to go back to school, but it wasn't possible. My mother had also fallen ill and my help was urgently needed in the shop, now run by my brothers. I was obliged to join them. I continued to help my brothers, serving customers and keeping the accounts, until I was twenty-four. In those days most girls would have been married by sixteen or eighteen. But I was needed at the store and nobody ever thought of finding me a husband until much later.

My memory is poor now. At times it's as though a big wind had blown straight through my head, shaken it like a tree and left only a few leaves behind. But I remember well the day I first met my future husband. My mother had taken me to have *yum cha* — to drink tea — with some relatives. There was nothing very special about this as our kinship was close and we saw each other often. But this time a stranger attended the party. And even though we were never introduced, I noticed that he watched me closely. It was only later that evening, after we had returned home, that my mother told me that the stranger had been chosen by my family as my future husband.

You know, I even remember what I wore that day. It was a black suit, the skirt long enough just to touch my ankles, the blouse buttoned high with a Chinese-style collar. It was silk, and blue flowers had been sewn onto the skirt, giving it a look of quiet elegance — or so my mother said. She had bought it at the Wing On department store for thirteen dollars, which in those days was quite a lot of money.

Soon after our first meeting the customary pre-wedding arrangements began. An auspicious date was chosen by the astrologer. Fung Tsun, my future husband, sent the *laisee* — money in red packets — to my mother, and to me he sent a gold wedding ring. Meanwhile my mother took me shopping for my dowry. We bought dresses, skirts, blouses and shoes, as well as pillows, blankets,

*Chan Ng*

bedspreads and many other items that might come in useful for my future household.

Neither of our families was very wealthy, so it was decided that the wedding celebrations would be simple. The night before the wedding I invited four or five of my friends to join me in a small party. We ate, drank, gossiped, giggled and had great fun until it was very late at night. So late that some of my friends decided not to return home and spent the night with us.

The next day, at noon, the matchmaker came to accompany me to my future home. I was introduced to each member of my husband's family and I made tea and bowed to all of them. My husband and I also paid respects to our ancestors. Later my friends came to join our families for dinner. As we were celebrating in modern style I didn't wear the traditional red *kwa*. Instead I wore a bright pink suit which was made of silk, with sea-blue trimmings. And I wore pink embroidered shoes. My hair was tied up in an S-shaped bun with a pink peony tucked behind my left ear. Yes, I looked a pretty bride. Fancy me remembering all this!

Unfortunately there is little I can recall or tell you about my married life and all that happened during those years. We led a very ordinary existence. My husband — he was four years older than me — was a salesman for an import-export firm. We had two daughters, both healthy and obedient girls. Many years ago both my daughters went back to the mainland because they couldn't find work in Hong Kong. But they were caught up in the civil war. And because they were afraid their background might get them into trouble with the Red soldiers of the People's Liberation Army they burned their Hong Kong birth certificates. It was very silly, but they were young and frightened.

Several years ago my husband died. I was all alone and applied for my daughters to come and join me in Hong Kong. But since they had no documents to prove their local birth they were refused admission. That's why I am here in this old people's home, all on my own. The fortune teller did not advise me well. Wai-ping was nothing but an empty promise. My name is Chan Ng!

# *The man who was different*

**M**y name is C.Y. Chong, ID card B-765632, Public Assistance recipient, Reference No. 9649. My Christian name is John.

I am overseas Chinese. I was born in Java on 12 September 1912. I am second generation Indonesian, but racially I am pure Chinese. Both my grandfather and my father married brides from China. Had they married ethnic Indonesians, all the other Chinese families would have looked down on them.

My grandfather was born in Amoy in the last century when everybody was poor and people were looking for opportunities abroad. When still young, he was told he could find work as a contract labourer in Java. After his family decided that he should go, he made the journey by sea with many other young men from Fukien Province. In the beginning, life was tough. But, as you know, we Chinese are hard-working and my grandfather was also very thrifty. Gradually he became a prosperous landowner and his son, my father, received a good education.

No, I have never been to our ancestral village. You must understand that we overseas Chinese have different customs, habits, culture, education and background. I am not trying to denigrate my Chinese relatives or boast about myself. I am talking facts. Back in China, they are mostly peasants, coolies, servants and — just maybe — shop attendants. They are uneducated, crass, and loud-mouthed. I had a higher education and have been the manager of a printing factory. No, we have nothing in common.

When I was seventeen, I was sent to university in Shanghai. I joined an undergraduate study programme and enrolled in business classes. Back home in Indonesia we owned a large coconut farm and I was expected to enter the business. But I never graduated; when the Japanese first attacked Shanghai, I was forced to leave university and return to Java. It was then that I had a difficult time. I had adapted to city ways and wasn't suited to the rough life of the countryside.

It was for that reason that I left Java to come to Hong Kong. My two brothers left as well. My elder brother went to Singapore where he died during the occupation. I don't know under what circumstances. My younger brother followed me to Hong Kong. He was killed by Japanese soldiers. How did it happen? As you must know, it was the rule in those days that you had to kowtow if you passed a Japanese soldier on the street. My brother failed to do so. I don't know whether it was because he didn't see the soldiers, or whether he objected to the rule. Anyhow, they hit him and kicked him viciously. He died a few days later. They were very cruel, the Japanese soldiers.

I knew how cruel they could be. You see, I had been conscripted by the Japanese and forced into hard labour — building roads and digging tunnels. Then they found out that I was an educated man. It was obvious, even to them, that I was different. From the way I spoke and moved, they could tell that I was not the ordinary type.

And so they found a different kind of work for me. I was employed as an interpreter and worked at the YMCA translating letters and documents. They paid me in both money and rice — I was really very lucky. Everywhere in Hong Kong people were starving. Many were skinny with swollen

*Chong Chan-yee*

bellies. My family and I had more than most and thus were able to survive.

Let me tell you about one strange incident. It was towards the end of the war, and, as many things were being stolen, the Japanese ordered me to make an inventory of the storeroom at the YMCA. And do you know what I found there? I found a gold bar! It must have been left there by the British and I wanted to keep it. But my wife scolded me. She said: 'Are you crazy? The Japanese are merciless. We have survived so long — why risk our lives now for a single bar of gold? Give it back to them.' I returned the bar. It was not an easy decision.

When the war ended, I found work as a printing broker. I solicited orders, referred them to the printing factories and was paid commission. I had lots of customers. Later, when I had some capital, I established my own business: a packaging and printing factory. My office was at Number 43 Mirador Mansion, second floor, in Tsimshatsui. My workshop was on Kam Shan Road near Taipo, beside the Lam river. The number of my business registration certificate was 39940.

In 1982 there were several days of heavy, continuous rainfall. My workshop was flooded. Everything I had — my machines, raw materials and finished products — were washed away in the river. I was not insured against natural disaster. Overnight I was destitute.

You can imagine my despair and the humiliation when I had to turn to Social Welfare for help. First they put me into a transit camp for homeless people; then I was given accommodation in a temporary housing hut. Finally, the Department arranged for me to be rehoused in a government housing estate. I had to share my room with two other men. One, as it turned out, was a good and sober man; the other was abnormal and half-crazed. He had a hot temper and was unbalanced. He was a Kung Fu expert with an aggressive nature who threatened me with an eight-inch knife. He kicked me around and, once, beat me up so badly that I had to stay in Queen Elizabeth Hospital for three days. The police did nothing.

Eventually, I was forced to move into a shelter for street sleepers. There I found myself sharing a room with beggars, cripples and all sorts of sickly outcasts. I could not bear the smell, the constant noise of coughing, spitting and retching. The environment was simply terrible. Worse still, I was put into the upper part of a double bunk bed, which I could hardly climb onto as I suffer from rheumatism, high blood pressure and diabetes. I was desperate.

In the end, I was offered accommodation in this hostel. This is not bad. But you must understand I am educated. I was a businessman — I am different. What I really want is a one-person flat in a government public housing unit. With a room of my own, then I would be content.

*Lung Sau-sing*

# *Sins and sorrows*

I was born in Kwangsi Province in 1910. My father was a commander of high rank in the army based in Canton. He fought against the Japanese, but he never surrendered as did that coward Long Chi-chuang. He died in battle and was a well-known hero in his day. Even now, people of my age remember him. His name was Lung Yau-hing.

When I was very young I overheard someone say to my mother 'What a pity that you didn't bear a son'. A son, you see, would have inherited my father's title. In those days women played only minor roles in society and were discriminated against. Nowadays it is certainly different. My father loved me though. I was his only child and the apple of his eye. Although I was young he taught me virtuous living and an abiding love for our glorious country. He was a man of high moral standards who set an example to others. People said that I took after him.

I am an educated woman. When I was a child a private tutor was employed to teach me the Four Books and classics at home. My father wouldn't let me attend a public school for fear I would make undesirable friends. But to tell you the truth, it was very dull at times and I was bored. Unlike other families, where children played with one another or with their cousins, I was all alone. But later, after the death of my father, our circumstances were greatly reduced and my mother had no choice but to allow me to attend school. I finished my education at the Sung Xing School in Nanning.

Until my father died our family lived in luxury. Our house was quite spectacular in those days — five storeys high and always guarded by soldiers. We employed at least eight servants and even owned a private car. Now that I am almost a beggar, that may seem like boasting and I feel shy to mention it. But you know, in the past, officers' families were usually very well off. I am still a bit choosy over my food even now, as I used to eat only the choicest delicacies. I was spoiled and I often feel that it is really a kind of punishment that now, at the end of my life, I am poor.

When my father was killed my mother was already quite ill. We were left land and other property, but women in those days were easily cheated and soon there was little left. My mother was worried that no one would take care of me after her death. For that reason she went to a matchmaker to arrange a marriage for me. I was married when I was seventeen, in the month of October. Four months later, at the end of January, my husband developed stomach pains. He became seriously ill. There was no hospital or surgeon nearby and he died. I was a widow after only four months of marriage. That was when life began to take a disastrous turn for me. No, I had no child by my husband. In those days people were much more shy than they are now. They didn't have children right after their marriage — let alone before, as people are doing nowadays.

After the death of my husband, his older brother took me to the home of my mother-in-law. My own mother, who was still alive, was terribly sad. But in those days it was obligatory for a widow to live with the family of her deceased husband. And they were genteel folk, a large and wealthy clan, and they treated me well. That is why I fulfilled my obligations to my mother-in-law and eventually, as the war spread, followed her to Hong Kong.

Then everything became like a nightmare. It is hard to imagine it now. My mother-in-law had borne eight sons and she lost them all during the war. Most of her daughters-in-law also disappeared. In the end, I was the only one left to care for her. How terrible, how sad. As for my own mother — I never saw her again. She was very ill and quite old when we lost touch. Surely she must be dead by now.

When I first came to Hong Kong I found employment looking after children. Later a niece introduced me to work at St Teresa's Hospital in Kowloon. Then the Japanese invaded Hong Kong and my mother-in-law and I took refuge in China — first in Kunming then in Chungking. Wherever we went the Japanese came and we were forced to escape and look for shelter elsewhere. In the end we went to Canton and stayed there. Times were really terrible. But I was young, strong and pretty. That is how we managed to survive.

You ask how we supported ourselves? Well, you must understand that in those days work was almost impossible to come by. People were starving and the enemy was everywhere. I heard that there was a gambling den on Fifteenth Street in Canton and it so happened that the organiser was a friend of my uncle's. I went to see him and he asked me what kind of salary I wanted. I told him I needed one catty of rice but he gave me cooking oil as well and a hundred dollars a week to buy sundries. He was a generous man. My mother-in-law did not approve of my job. I didn't like it either; but I was young and beautiful and there were few alternatives. They employed eight women and I was the prettiest of them all.

My duties? You might say that I was a sort of accountant. And that is what got me into real trouble! Only a week after I had started working there the police closed the den and I was arrested. They came with sirens blaring in two cars. I begged them not to handcuff me because people would misunderstand and mistake me for a prostitute. The police felt sorry for me. They said I had the looks of an educated lady but that they couldn't help. I was taken to the police station to be questioned and finally I was detained in prison overnight. I was so ashamed! There had been tax evasion and I was thought to be responsible. But I had worked there for only one week and the place was licensed. I had every document to prove my innocence.

Next morning my boss came to bail me out. He told me not to worry because my mother-in-law was being well cared for. He was extremely pleased that I had not given evidence against him during the investigations. To tell the truth, people spent large sums of money betting on numbered chips which were called white and red swallows, but I told the detectives that customers were allowed to gamble only up to a maximum of fifty dollars. They believed me, and as a result my boss was liable for a fine of only three thousand dollars.

Soon after the war I returned to Hong Kong. Through family connections I was given employment at St Teresa's Hospital again. From former days I had much experience with children so I was put to work in the children's ward. I worked very hard and the matron, who was French, was most impressed with my efforts. She promised me promotion. My prospects were excellent. Unfortunately she was unexpectedly obliged to return to France and you know how it is — 'Every sovereign brings his own courtiers'. I was dismissed. I was disappointed and felt that I should not apply for hospital work any more. So I became a private nurse and worked until I was sixty-six years old. Then my health began to deteriorate. Finally I was issued with a medical certificate stating that I was unfit to work. Now the government and some very generous people take care of me.

But I must apologise for having kept you. I have wasted a great deal of your valuable time with my useless story. You see, I am normally too shy to talk to others. I am afraid that they will not believe what I tell them. As you know, I am an educated woman. I have always known right from wrong. I always knew that it was evil to smoke, drink or gamble. People often ask me to join them playing mahjong. But now I never do. After I was baptised in the Catholic Church last Easter, I found a new purpose in life. Now I read the Bible so that I don't have time to think about my past sins and sorrows. I will accept any suffering until I enter the Kingdom of God. I'll do as my Lord tells me.

# *Tricks of fate*

**T**he last hundred years in China have been turbulent. Family fortunes have changed suddenly and dramatically. Myself, I have had a bad time of it and so have many of my generation.

Look at these photographs; you can hardly recognise me now, can you? When I lived in China, I was so thin that I looked older than I do even now. Our daily rice ration was less than three taels per person — not even enough for one bowl. So I really had to leave China, if only to survive. That was in 1967.

My children, on the other hand, are doing fine on the mainland now. I have three: two boys and one girl. Both boys used to be farmers and were barely making a living. Now things have changed and they work as small-time hawkers. They live in our native village in their own houses which were passed on to our family through my grandfather. My sons now have most things they need. For them it has all come good in the end.

I come from a place called Chungshan which is not far from here. My father was a farmer — not a rich landlord but not poor either. He married only once and my mother bore him thirteen children of whom I was the ninth. But only five grew up to marry. I am eighty-five this year.

I first came to Hong Kong when I was fourteen to join an aunt on my mother's side. Because I had some education I found work at the Wing On department store as an errand boy. Later I was promoted to sell merchandise. But when I was eighteen I did a stupid thing. I left Hong Kong and went to Macau where I had been offered a job as a cashier in a restaurant. I say I was stupid because I gave up a steady job in a good company with good prospects of promotion. Also, Macau is really a backward place. Still, I earned good money. The basic salary was only about forty dollars a month; but there were bonuses and, altogether, I took home about a hundred dollars a month.

At that time there was a girl from Shuntak County who took an interest in me. Her father was a coffin-maker and his shop was just across the street from the restaurant of my employer. The two knew one another well. Anyhow, she used to come and ask for my help with calculations — using the abacus and things like that. Then her mother died and my employer suggested that I should marry the girl. To be honest, I didn't really want to get married at that time, nor to her. But my employer put pressure on me and in the end I agreed.

It was the new style of marriage: she brought along no dowry and we had no tea ceremony. However, we did pay respects to our ancestors. Actually, my wife had some money of her own; but, being of the modern generation, we did not want to use it on a lavish wedding. We decided to save it as we were thinking of emigrating.

Well, as I have said, I was young and foolhardy in those days. And yes, once again I did something very stupid. I quit my work at the restaurant and took a job on a ship going to New York. I had no interest in becoming a sailor, you understand. I planned to jump ship and enter the United States illegally. Many had done it before me — it was popular to go to America in those days. But as it turned out I never got there. We were in Calcutta when our crew got involved in

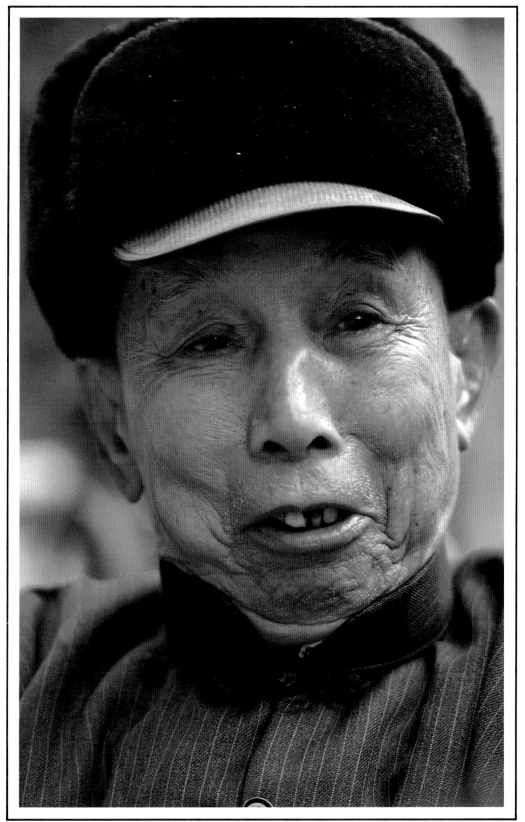

*Ho Man-bun*

a big fight. Someone was killed and several of us were sent back to Shanghai. Fate plays rough tricks on us, doesn't it?

Well, I was stranded in Shanghai and my wife came to join me. But it was no good. The Wing On company — as you may know, they had a large store in Shanghai — wouldn't give me a job. Back to Hong Kong, and then to Macau, but there were no jobs there either. Finally I returned to Chungshan where I had to turn to my parents to support me. Then both my mother and father died, as well as my older and younger brothers. That was in 1942 in the thirty first year of the Republic in the terrible famine during the Japanese war.

My wife had died in her early thirties and my children were living with her relatives in Shuntak at that time. So eventually I decided to try my luck in Hong Kong once more. I had to walk back carefully, avoiding the main roads because of the 'Turnip-heads' — that's what we called the Japanese. It took me three weeks to walk to Hong Kong. When I arrived I was horribly dirty and covered in lice. I had to take some very lowly jobs just to survive.

In 1949 China was 'liberated'. In the beginning nobody knew quite what to make of it. People said this, people said that. But then I heard that life was improving there. People told me that with my experience I would get good points under the new work system. The government was changing society and, they said, everyone would get a decent living. But, of course, it didn't work out like that. In the beginning, when I first went back, I worked as an accountant — and I just scraped by. But the Communists hadn't really started yet. It wasn't until 1957 that they began to change our lives in earnest.

You have some knowledge, I expect, about Chairman Mao's communes, but knowing about something is different from experiencing it. First we were all banded together. We were shoved into work teams, brigades and communes. We had to work together and we had to eat together. But eating was a joke — there was hardly any food. Everyone had just one bowl of *congee* a meal. Farming was in a very bad way. Although in our village nobody actually died of starvation, we were always hungry. The children got swollen bellies.

Then came the Great Leap Forward and, with it, small local industrial production. Things got steadily worse. Then in 1966 the Great Proletarian Cultural Revolution spread across China. Red Guards were all over the streets and forced us to read the works of Chairman Mao. We had to attend political meetings almost every day. Those of us who had some education were spat upon.

This time I had had enough. I just couldn't take it any more. A nephew, the son of one of my brothers, was in Hong Kong and I applied to join him. Because I was already elderly and therefore considered useless to China, I was readily given permission to leave and I returned to Hong Kong in 1968. I worked until a few months ago when I hurt my leg and had to stop.

I have children, grandchildren and great grandchildren who remain in China. I went for a visit last Lunar New Year but I can't afford to go again this year. I have not got the money for presents — and visitors from Hong Kong simply can't go home empty-handed!

# *Second daughter of the fourth concubine*

Our village was big. It had four gates and our family lived by the East Gate. There were so many of us that I can't recall the total number, but I think there must have been more than a hundred family members. Because there were so many children in the house, we never went out to play. A tutor was hired to teach us all to read and write. The girls were taught as well.

When I was young my father's eldest brother was the head of the family. He had married at the age of sixteen and had taken a concubine when he was eighteen. He had three sons and two daughters. He died young. My father's wife was the daughter of an official in Shumchun, near Hong Kong. She was educated but she could not bear children. We had a big house in Canton and she lived there. Sometime during the last decade of the nineteenth century my father went to Peking to take the Imperial Examination. He passed with Honours but refused an appointment in the south and was sent to work somewhere near Peking. It was then that he took his first concubine.

I was born in 1900, the second daughter of my father's fourth concubine. He took five altogether and fathered eleven sons and five daughters. When I was quite small and too young to study, I was taken from the village to live in our house in Canton for a while. The concubines would take turns to go to Canton to look after the children there. My father's wife was very kind to them. She was good-natured and didn't mind when the concubines spoiled the children.

When his elder brother died, my father came back from the north to look after the family property. We were quite rich. We had twenty-one tenant farmers and also owned a rice shop. My father was a generous man who made many charitable donations. But at home he was very strict. Although he would play chess with his old friends, he did not allow any gambling in his house — not even among his concubines.

My father was also very conservative. He had a queue and he refused to have it cut off. 'What good is it to have loose hair all over the face?' he said. 'So much tidier to keep it in a plait.' Even after the Revolution my father forbade his children to cut their hair. My eldest brother went to Canton to study and was forced by his fellow students to cut off his queue. He was severely scolded when he came home. A granddaughter, also at school in Canton, cut off her hair because all the other girls at school had cut theirs off. She was so scared that she didn't come home for the New Year. My father asked 'Why is Ah Sheung not here to celebrate with us?' We told him she was busy studying. We didn't dare tell him the truth.

My father died before I left home. The property was divided between the sons, and the concubines were all guaranteed food for life. They were quite fortunate. Our great grandfather had left some land which was not allowed to be sold and the income supported the concubines and the poorer members of the house. This was to protect the family against irresponsible sons who might gamble and lose everything.

We were so fortunate when I was young. We had a tailor and two seamstresses in the house and because there were so many of us they were always busy. We didn't have to do our own

*Tang Yick-foon*

sewing, but the seamstresses taught me embroidery and how to make Chinese buttons. We also had many bond-maids; each wife and each daughter had one. Now I am over eighty and I do everything myself. We never had to do anything when I was a girl.

I was married at eighteen. It was an arranged marriage and celebrated in the traditional way. I had no say in it; my mother made all the arrangements. On the wedding day I was carried in a bridal sedan-chair to my husband's house. I took gold and pearls as my dowry. My husband was a teacher. We lived in Canton. He died when I was twenty-four but we had no children. So I returned to my husband's village to live with my in-laws. That was my duty. Later my in-laws died and I went to stay with my sister's family in the countryside. But then both my sister and her husband also died and I was left to look after their son, who was two years old then.

When my nephew reached thirteen I arranged for him to go to Hong Kong as an apprentice. I remember it well. He left on the third day of the New Year and on the fourth day the border was closed. I had stayed behind in the village to sort things out before going to Hong Kong myself. But when I arrived at the border I was stopped and not allowed to join him. What was I to do? Those were hard times! My nephew is a good boy. He stayed with an uncle and qualified as an engine fitter. When he had finished his apprenticeship he was earning less than a hundred dollars a month, but still he sent money to me and other relatives in the village.

When I was sixty-two my nephew applied for me to come to Hong Kong. He said he would look after me, but because he worked and slept in a shop I had to stay in a rented room by myself. My nephew brought plastic flowers for me to assemble, but otherwise there was nothing to do and life was boring. I came to this home because my rent was put up and I could no longer pay for food. My nephew is married now and has one child. He is working very hard, but he is poor. I have told him not to bring his family too often because transport costs are so high.

My grandnephew came from Canton to see me here and said 'You are quite well off; this is not bad'. I said: 'Here I am, over eighty and living in an old folk's home. Am I not to be pitied? Why should I not weep?' He said: 'No, you mustn't think like that. How can you think of the past? After all, you used to have dozens of maids and many servants. Didn't they serve you day and night? You didn't even have to get your hands wet. They would wring your handcloth for you to wipe your fingers. Life was too easy. No point in thinking about the past. This is not bad!'

*Cheng Hei*

# *Chiuchow smuggler*

**I** am a Chiuchow man, from Swatow. I was born in the Year of the Ram and I'm now eighty-six. My father was a teacher of the martial arts; he was big and tall like a Shantung fellow, well respected and sometimes feared. I can read a bit. My father made me study under a Ching Scholar. But the problem was that I refused to work. When I was still quite young my teacher sent me home. He told my folks there was no point in giving me an education.

I was thirteen when my parents sent me to Hong Kong where I've done various jobs. What sort of work? Too many years have passed. My memory is dim, I can't remember much about the early times. For a while I had a job as an office boy. Later, when I was about thirty, I was fixed up with work as a seaman by a Chiuchow man like myself — I'll just call him Mr Wong. I worked on the Singapore-Hong Kong run and also did trips between Hong Kong and Shanghai. I stayed at sea for thirty years, always with the same company.

My job was that of a foreman, accounting for all the cargo received and delivered. We used to do a lot of smuggling in those days. During the war, we took materials for the Japanese to Shanghai. Mr Wong, who later became a director of a large bank, made a lot of money out of those deals. On one occasion we were actually caught and Mr Wong paid me to go to court, pretending I was him. He also paid for a good lawyer and got me acquitted. Had I gone to prison, I would have been well looked after.

When I was sixty, the Union would not allow me to go to sea any more. I was refused a medical certificate and forced to retire. But I still needed work to support myself and my family. So I went to see Mr Wong at his bank. I had been Mr Wong's *matsai*, or henchman, for nearly fifty years — anything he told me to do, I did it — so he had an obligation to help me. I went to him and said, 'I can't go to sea any more. You must give me rice to eat. The best thing would be if I became a watchman.'

So he gave me employment as a caretaker/watchman at a warehouse in Aberdeen. I got a salary of $800 a month and a place to sleep as well. It was a 'ghost' job, as there was no real work to do. I stayed there for seven or eight years until I was asked to retire because of my age. Mr Wong gave me three thousand dollars and told me to go back to my family in China. I didn't like the life in China so I asked the Social Welfare Department for help. That's why I'm in this home now.

Life is not bad. My family lives in Swatow. I have one son, one daughter and two grandchildren — both boys. What I'd really like is to apply for them to come and join me here. Then I'd be happy.

# *A bargain bride*

I came to Hong Kong in 1945 when I was thirty-three. My own family was very poor. My parents had about ten children but only five of us survived. I saw my eldest brother starve to death during the Japanese war. A great pity for he was doing well at school. Later four more of us children died of starvation. Now I have three brothers, and a sister, in the village.

I was married at sixteen — one less to feed. It was a blind marriage and my husband paid the *muiyan*, or go-between, only one hundred dollars. Can't say I was expensive, eh? At twenty-five I was a widow. Until then I had been just a housewife working at home, helping my husband a little. But after about eight years my husband went to Vietnam to try to set up a business. He died there a year later. He had never sent much money home, so I was still poor.

When the Japanese invaded our village, I could barely look after myself. I did some buying and selling of medicinal herbs, just as my husband had done. I was often pushed around and even beaten by the Japanese. But I was more afraid of starving than of the Japanese, so I carried on. One of my brothers — he was only in his teens — followed the Japanese to Vietnam to build sampans. He worked only for his meals; I don't know how the others survived.

When I came to Hong Kong, I had an uncle living in Shaukeiwan. First I worked in the factories, then I became a baby amah. I worked for four or five families and looked after many children. But they have all forgotten me now. No one has kept in touch. Don't think it's a soft life looking after children. You never get enough sleep. Employers are fussy and demanding. Food is not all that great either. I used to eat with the children. It's a pity I could never be a wet-nurse. They get better treatment. Of course, my employers provided me with clothes; every year I would be given a new pair of black trousers and a white jacket. I even went out in chauffeur-driven cars, but I didn't like that a bit — I get car-sick. I had to watch over the children at the beach. Didn't like that either. I was really scared of the water as I couldn't swim.

As you know, some amahs have got quite rich from buying shares. I saved hard when I was a maid and bought myself some gold teeth and jewellery, but I never bought shares. I earned only about fifty dollars at first, then one hundred, two hundred and three hundred. I had to send some back to the village to my sister and brothers. When I was working I bought a hut and let somebody else stay there. That was about 1956; but then there was a fire and my hut went overnight. I paid over ten thousand dollars for that hut in Wongtaisin. I never lived in it; it was burned down ten days after I bought it.

I used to be a Buddhist but now I've lost interest in religion. In fact, I don't have many interests left; I just watch TV. Yes, I have been back to my village a few times to see my sister and brothers. And yes, they are reasonably well; most of them are retired but one brother is still building boats. They don't give me any money; they have barely enough to eat. I used to take old clothes back to them and food when I could afford it. They've asked me to stay with them. But for now, I prefer to remain in Hong Kong.

*Chan How-chun*

# *I did what I could*

**M**y birthplace was the market town of Waiyeung, east of Canton — about two and a half days away from the city if you were walking during the daylight hours, but closer by riverboat. I was the youngest in a family of four children. We all worked selling salt, buying it from the miners and carrying it for hours to the central market. When there was heavy rain we couldn't work, because the salt would spoil. We were a poor family and, being Hakkas, belonged to a minority in the town. We were liable to be pushed around by the Hoklo and Chiuchow people.

Schooling? Not for the likes of us. It cost eighty cents a year in fees and that was more than my father could afford. You see, there wasn't even money to buy pork or extra food at the New Year. We children got the Hakka *laisee*, nine copper coins with a hole in the centre tied up with red string. And that was all. On normal days we would usually manage to eat twice a day, starting with rice at eight in the morning. If money was short we would make do with a bowl of *congee*.

My father died when I was fifteen; that was in 1922. It became very difficult to make ends meet. First both my brothers and my sister set off for Hong Kong where they hoped to find work. A couple of years later I went to Canton where I found work as a waiter; room and board plus a dollar a month which I used to send home to my mother. Some time in the Twenties, my boss went out of business. I found work first in a grocery store, then in a coffee-shop. By this time I had brought my mother to live with me.

You were safer in the really big towns during the Twenties. In a market town like Waiyeung there was constant trouble from bandits and warlords' troops. Whenever the soldiers came we would run and hide in the hills. Well, then the Japanese came. My mother fell ill and died, so I decided to clear off to Hong Kong.

When I got here, I looked for my brothers and sister. We had been separated for years, without ever hearing from each other. But although I inquired everywhere in Hong Kong, I never found them. I asked among Hakka people, in the villages as well as in town. But nothing, no news. Then I picked up a story — no more than a rumour really — that they had been bonded somewhere to tobacco-leaf suppliers. Gone to work on the plantations overseas? I don't know, anyway it was only a rumour. I never found out what happened to them.

Married? Yes, I was married just before coming to Hong Kong. Of course, an arranged marriage! The village elders decided it. The girl's name, date and hour of birth were written on red paper and this was put on our family altar. And since for three days nothing bad happened — like breaking a bowl, or something similar — the girl was said to be OK and the marriage went ahead. I never saw a picture of her beforehand. She was just pointed out to me walking between the houses. 'There! That's the one you'll be marrying.'

It happens like this. When an important man in the village wants to get his daughter married, he inquires about the young men; who are the bad characters, who are the reliable fellows. Well, I didn't smoke or drink or gamble so they picked me and gave me no peace until I agreed to marry

*Yip Sang*

the girl. And you know, she wasn't half bad after all!

We had just about settled in Hong Kong when the Japanese came here as well. Survive? Like everyone else, I did what I could: peddling food in the streets, selling dried fish and vegetables, selling cigarettes — the genuine kind and the fakes, made of banana leaf. Somehow we scraped by.

The Japanese gave me this bad back. I was passing the checkpoint at Tsuenwan, carrying vegetables and wearing a big straw hat. And I forgot to touch the brim of the hat and bow. So as I passed they bashed me across the back with a club. I can still feel it but it doesn't worry me that much any more.

I worked hawking vegetables on the streets until I was seventy. Then I built a wooden hut in Tsuenwan where I opened a tea and coffee stall for workers on the building sites nearby. But later I developed heart trouble and had to go to hospital, and finally I was recommended to this home.

We had four children and two of them have survived. There's my son, aged forty-three, who married a Thai girl; and there's my daughter — her husband works in a dyeing factory. I see them sometimes. My first wife died long ago, and my second wife is gravely ill. I'm eighty-two now. The happiest time of my life? Happiness? I'm not sure I know what you mean.

# *Why am I here?*

**A**ll I want is to go back to Vietnam to find my son. He's grown-up, yes, but he needs me because he's mentally handicapped. All his life I was there to give him special care. I don't know how he's managing without me. And my existence here is just pointless. I can do no work — I can hardly even move around since I had that fall and broke my hip. I have no one in Hong Kong except a stepdaughter, and she's far too poor to look after me. I should never have come. If I'd known, I would never have agreed to leave Vietnam.

It's been twelve or thirteen years now since I came to Hong Kong, when things were looking bad in Saigon. My eldest son — who was looking after the family business — had been arrested by the Communists and nothing was heard of him again. My daughters and other relatives urged me to leave because I was getting old and they were afraid things might get too rough for me. They said that if I went first, and joined my stepdaughter in Hong Kong, they would be able to hang on and judge the situation without having to worry about me. And we would be reunited, either here or back home, later on. But that's the last I've seen of my family. I miss them so much, especially my youngest son.

At first I lived in hope and waited. I got work — I didn't mind doing menial jobs and living modestly, although I hadn't expected life to be so hard here. But as the years wore on, and there was still no word from Vietnam, I felt more and more like an exile, stranded all alone. It was just the last straw when I fell and hurt myself in the rain when I was going home from work in the factory. And now I'm disabled.

I don't know that I really want to talk about my younger days — is there any point in talking about the past? But it's very good of you to take an interest. Yes, I have a Vietnamese name now, but I was born in Fatshan, near Canton. It was 1918. I was the treasured daughter of a well-to-do family. Then I was married to a wonderful man whose family had a prosperous trading business. We were very happy but, as with everyone else, things became grim for us during the Japanese war. Then there were the Communists, and when it became clear that they were going to take over we decided to move to Vietnam. We were already doing a lot of business with Vietnam, so moving there seemed a logical thing.

Oh, Vietnam was such a beautiful place then! The rice fields stretched as far as you could see and the rice ripened so fast. Everything grew so fast and luscious there. We were in the import-export trade and we carried on a jewellery business on the side. There was quite a clan of us and we all lived together in a large family house. It was a three-storey house with plenty of ground around it. The main hall was so large that it could easily fit in twelve round tables — which we always had at celebration dinners. And there were many servants to look after us.

But then came a dreadful blow — my husband died. And I was only thirty-nine. I didn't know what to do. Our eldest child was only nine or ten years old. People suggested that I should remarry, and my in-laws were very sympathetic. But I didn't remarry — my children wouldn't let me! They clung to me and pleaded with me not to. So I decided to stay and see things through. And for the

*Ngo Hue Khanh*

next thirty years I took on the responsibilities which would have been my husband's, as head of the family. It was very hard during the war. The countryside was devastated — hardly any crops were produced. And it was often necessary to do all kinds of jobs in order to keep our business going. But we managed it. When the Communists came though, our business really dwindled and then our property was confiscated. And finally they arrested my eldest son.

People are very kind to me here in this home. I get two simple meals a day — but I can't get them down because I keep asking myself what's the point. Why am I here? What am I doing in this place? How am I to end this mess as I face old age? I just can't resign myself to it — this isn't what life is about. If I could only return to Vietnam and find my youngest son, who needs me. If we could face life together, then I should feel blessed. I wouldn't mind how harsh life was. At least I would be where I should be.

*Wong Bin-lam*

# *A tough bunch*

I grew up by myself in Chiuchow City in the county of Chiu On. My mother died soon after I was born in 1918, so I don't remember anything about her. My father worked on ocean-going ships and he was often away. I lived in hostels with Chiuchow workmen. We Chiuchow stick together and help each other.

When my father decided to move to Hong Kong I tried to get a job as a coolie unloading cargo on Kowloon side. But I was too young and skinny and the foremen wouldn't even look at me. The other coolies, all Chiuchow, let me live with them in a six-storey hostel building on Haiphong Road. I earned some money as a shoeshine boy at the Star Ferry. But you don't get rich at shining shoes, believe me. On average I would only get three pairs to shine in a whole day — at five cents a pair. But I could live on it. In those days, a plate of restaurant leftovers was only two cents.

When I was about eighteen I finally got a job as a coolie — unloading all sorts of cargo onto the railway trucks, one or two tons to a truck. I worked with a team of other coolies pushing the trucks to the main door of the warehouse. The pay then was fifteen dollars a month and I did that job for thirty years. I used to play mahjong with the other fellows — but not for high stakes. Sometimes I'd watch opera. I married a Chiuchow girl when I was twenty-one and we had a son and a daughter. Those were the best times. Then the war came and changed everything. My wife and children were killed when the Allies bombed Hunghom in Kowloon where we had a flat.

When I was getting old, and couldn't do heavy work any more, I took a job on a construction site guarding the heavy equipment. I stayed there every night for five years until one night, very late, robbers broke in. They were escaping with some tools. I climbed a wire fence to try to head them off, but I fell and injured my leg very seriously. I ended up in hospital in a bad way. They wanted to amputate, but I wasn't going to lose my leg. I refused. I simply refused!

So eventually they telephoned the Catholic priest here and said that they had an injured man who refused an operation and would he take me? And that is how I came here. Yes, it's true, I walk askew with a bad limp; but isn't that better than losing your leg? You think I've had a tough life? Well, I don't know. I'm Chiuchow, you see; we're a tough bunch.

# Sometimes, at night, I cry

On the fourth day of the fourth lunar month eighty-two years ago, I was born in a small village in Chungshan County, far from any big town. About a hundred families lived there together, growing vegetables and collecting firewood to sell in the market. Some people in the village had a little money which they gave to relatives who left to go overseas; but the rest of us were poor and life was hard for all of us.

I had two older sisters and one day, when I was still a young girl, a matchmaker came to our house. My mother lined up the three of us and, to my amazement, she picked me as the one to get married. I really hadn't expected this and it was quite a shock. We didn't know the boy at all and he turned out to be even poorer than we were. Worse luck for me!

After I was married, I gave birth to two sons in three years. That was enough for me. I didn't want any more children because my husband was useless. He worked for a relative in a shop and received two meals a day — but almost no pay. He was a gambler and didn't really provide for his family. I looked after the children as best I could with the help of my mother. She would bring food and take care of us when I was pregnant. Without her, we would not have survived.

My husband died when our sons were eight and six. To support them I became a street hawker. Walking and squatting, I would sell salted fish from a rattan basket and peddle pickled vegetables in the village. When I made money, we all ate rice; when I didn't, I'd feed the children rice and I would eat sweet potatoes. My elder son helped me, so I couldn't send him to school. We did manage to send his brother, who learned to read and write.

One day, when I was out in the fields picking vegetables, bombs began to fall on the village. I stuffed as much food as I could into my clothes and ran back to our house. A bomb had fallen into the firewood which was stacked alongside the house and had started a blaze. Some neighbours came to help put out the fire, but the house was badly damaged. Shortly after, Japanese soldiers came to the village and everyone who could fled to the neighbouring village. I took refuge with my mother until the soldiers had gone.

When the war with Japan ended, the civil war began. We were luckier this time because there was no fighting around our village; but still there was no food. Everyone was allowed just four taels of rice a day. With only twelve taels between us, my sons and I were always hungry. Later things improved a bit under the Communists. They divided up the land and gave each of us a portion on which to grow vegetables. Because we were poor peasants they didn't bother us much and we were left alone.

It was at this time that my two sisters left to work in Hong Kong. They kept writing urging me to join them there. They were amahs for rich families and promised to find work for me. But I didn't want to go. Life was getting better in China; my sons were older and we had enough to eat. Besides, my mother kept telling me bad stories about Hong Kong. How people had no place to live. How you could find work, eat well, but at night you would have nowhere to sleep. Hong Kong people were rude, she said, always in a rush. And there was also crime and prostitution. So

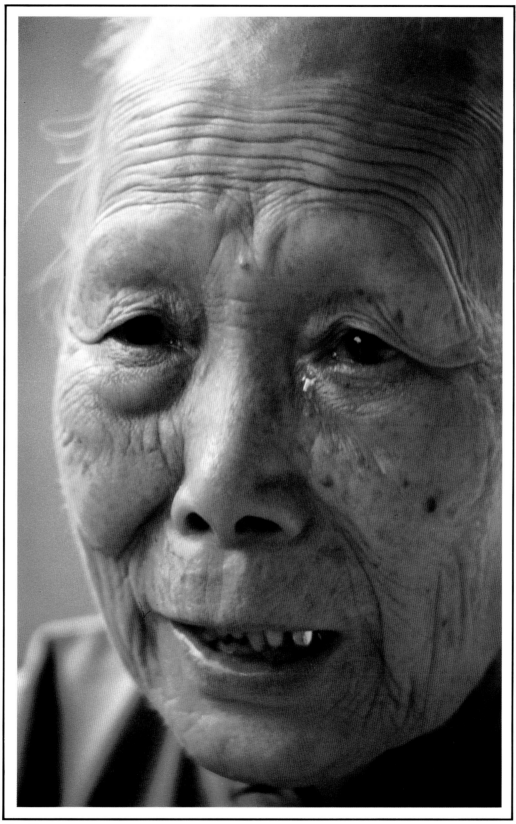

*Chan King-ngan*

I thought, why should I go there? And I really didn't want to leave my village.

Then my older son was married and he and his wife wanted to have children. So I thought, maybe now I should go to Hong Kong, make some money and send it home so that my son can fix up the house and raise a family. When I first arrived in Hong Kong I was already sixty years old. My sisters found me a job making plastic flowers. Later I became a packer earning three dollars a day. I was very careful with my money and sent back as much as I could, as my second son had also married and started a family.

When I was seventy I changed jobs. I became a cook in a factory preparing meals for the workers. Then, when I was seventy-eight, my arm gave out. My employer suggested that I should retire, go back to China and live with my sons. I went back, got my arm treated, then returned to Hong Kong to look for another job. But I couldn't find one. Who would hire a seventy-eight year old grandmother with a shaky arm? I had to apply for Public Assistance.

Do you know, I have only just realised that I have lived in Hong Kong for twenty-two years already. My sons are still in China, but my sisters and my godson come to visit me here in the old folk's hostel. My days are untroubled now; but as I look back and remember how bitter my life has been — then sometimes, at night, I cry.

# *Historical background*

| | | | |
|---|---|---|---|
| **1911** | Ching Dynasty overthrown by Revolution. | **1949** | Communists, led by Mao Tse-tung, defeat Nationalists. People's Republic of China (PRC) proclaimed. Chiang Kai-shek withdraws to Taiwan. |
| **1912** | Kuomintang (National People's Party, or KMT) founded by Sun Yat-sen. | | |
| **1920** | Chinese Communist Party formed. | **1950** | Korean War starts. Hong Kong hit by UN embargo on trade with China. |
| **1920** | Intermittent but widespread civil strife in China, continuing until 1949, with sporadic military campaigns by provincial warlords and hostilities, interspersed with truces, between Nationalists (KMT) and Communists. | **1952** | 'Three Antis' and 'Five Antis' campaigns in China. Targets for suppression included greed, waste, bureaucracy, shoddy production and other economic 'crimes'. |
| **1925** | Death of Sun Yat-sen. | **1958** | Great Leap Forward in China. Collectivisation of farming and 'backyard industrialisation', followed by famine in many areas. |
| **1928** | Chiang Kai-shek, as leader of KMT, sets up National Government of Republic of China. | | |
| **1931** | Japanese occupy Manchuria, beginning a gradual takeover of northern China. | **1960** | Sino-Soviet rift becomes public. |
| **1934** | Communists' Long March. | **1966** | Cultural Revolution in China, touching off riots in Hong Kong in 1967. |
| **1937** | Further invasion by Japanese, who take Peking, Shanghai and (the then capital) Nanking. | **1971** | China admitted to UN. US recognises PRC two years later. |
| **1938** | Japanese take Canton. | **1975** | Death of Chiang Kai-shek. |
| **1941** | Hong Kong invaded and occupied by Japanese. | **1976** | Death of Mao Tse-tung. |
| | | **1978** | Deng Xiao-ping comes to power in China, introducing modernisation programmes and steps towards a freer economy. |
| **1945** | Japan defeated by Allies. Liberation of Hong Kong. Waves of refugees from China begin to flood into Hong Kong. | **1984** | Sino-British Agreement on Hong Kong, providing for a transfer of sovereignty in 1997. |

## Ethnic minorities

The majority of the population of mainland Kwangtung are Han Chinese, speaking Cantonese dialects. For more than five hundred years there have been successive movements of people into the area. The ethnic groups mentioned in this collection of life-stories include the following.

**Hakka** — The Hakka, or 'guest' people, originally came from northern and central China. They are thought to have begun to settle in the area of the Pearl River delta in the fourteenth century, with many coming in by way of Fukien and Kiangsi provinces.

**Hoklo** — Another immigrant group who started to enter the Kwangtung area somewhat later than the Hakkas.

**Chiuchow** — People from Swatow, the main port-city of eastern Kwangtung, and the surrounding area. They have a seafaring tradition and many have emigrated to other countries.

**Tanka** — Loosely called 'sea gypsies', the Tanka people comprise a sizeable proportion of Hong Kong's now dwindling population of boat-dwellers.

All these groups have their own dialects, but all use standard Cantonese also.

This book has been produced to introduce to the people of Hong Kong some of the men and women whom they have so generously supported during the ten years of Helping Hand's history.

伸手助人協會
Helping Hand

SINKIANG

INNER M

NINGSIA

TSINGHAI

KANSU

SHEN

Chengtu

TIBET

SZECHWAN

Chungking

KWEICHOW

Kunming

YUNNAN

KWA

Na

VIETNAM